T0329435

Migration from Malawi to South Africa:
A Historical & Cultural Novel
Real-life Experiences

Harvey C. Chidoba Banda

Langaa Research & Publishing CIG
Mankon, Bamenda

Publisher:

Langaa RPCIG
Langaa Research & Publishing Common Initiative Group
P.O. Box 902 Mankon
Bamenda
North West Region
Cameroon
Langaagrp@gmail.com
www.langaa-rpcig.net

Distributed in and outside N. America by African Books Collective
orders@africanbookscollective.com
www.africanbookscollective.com

ISBN-10: 9956-763-95-0

ISBN-13: 978-9956-763-95-5

Dedication

For:

Migrants and Traders.
For their relentless fight against poverty in Malawi
through commercial and labour migration!

Table of Contents

Acknowledgements

This book is a product of my determination to document some of the experiences of labour migrants and traders from Malawi to South Africa, especially since the early 1990s. Although my encounter with these labour migrants and traders goes back to the early 1990s, the book is largely a product of the many trips I made from 2015 to 2017 between Malawi and South Africa as part of my PhD studies at the University of the Witwatersrand. I made most of these trips using coaches and this gave me a rare opportunity to personally interact with a cross-section of the labour migrants and traders of Malawi origin. Although, initially, my interaction with these labour migrants and traders was intended to understand the nature of migration between Malawi and South Africa particularly during the post-1990 period, gradually I broadened my scope and wanted to understand more broadly the experiences of these two categories of migrants not only in South Africa, but from the source (Malawi), during transit (their journey experiences), and, ultimately, their experiences upon arrival in their destination (South Africa).

For my ability to put pen to paper on these Malawian migrants' experiences, I am indebted to the numerous labour migrants and traders who I personally interviewed, both formally and informally, aboard the coaches and during brief stoppages between Malawi and South Africa. As in most research work and the resultant publications, it remains a pity and my heart-felt concern that the majority of these informants will not have a chance to read this book. Nonetheless, all I can say is '*nawonga chomene chifukwa chakujipereka kwinu mnyengo yichoko apa tikayendanga kuluta kweniso kufuma kula ku South*

Africa' (I remain grateful for your willingness to talk to me in the midst of busyness as we were traveling either to or from South Africa). I do not take this for granted, not in the least bit!

Last but not least, I am extremely grateful to my family, both immediate and 'at large', for their patience and tolerance of my frequent absences from home. I did most of my studies within Malawi and, therefore, my absences were not as prolonged as this one. Being full-time, my PhD studies virtually separated me from my family: my wife (Jennifer), son (Owen), brothers and sisters. Above all, I went away when my ageing parents needed me most; quite a difficult period. I remain thankful for their rare understanding.

Preface

This book, a historical novel, takes a unique format that is in many ways different from the usual history books. In writing the book, I have combined two approaches: first, that adopted in writing novels and pacesetters where the writer writes about occurrences but largely relying on his or her imaginations (the literary approach); and, second, that adopted by traditional historians in reconstructing the past where effort is made to document what exactly happened in the past (the historical approach). In adopting the first approach I have largely presented the labour migrants' and traders' experiences as some kind of fiction. But, in actual sense, what I have included in the book has no bearing on fiction *per se*; it is a record of what these migrants continue to experience as they travel to, and stay in, South Africa, hence the adoption of the historical approach. However, the names I have used throughout the book are fictitious. This is deliberately done to conceal the real identities of the labour migrants and traders I interviewed, especially aboard buses to and from South Africa. Some of the issues discussed in the book are sensitive and highly confidential and the best I could have done is not to put my 'benefactors' (labour migrants and traders) into problems by revealing their true identities. This is in line with the aim behind this book: to inform the readers about what exactly the migrants experience as they try to fulfil their respective migration goals, viz, wage employment and cross-border trade.

The second approach used in this book, the historical approach, has a bearing on the approach advanced by Leopold von Ranke (1795-1886). Ranke was a German historian and a founder of modern source-based history. Put differently,

Ranke has been praised as the originator of modern *scientific history*. Leopold von Ranke's famous dictum is that historians should represent the past "*wie es eigentlich gewesen*" (as it actually happened or 'tell ye as it was'). This statement sounds simple and matter-of-course, but it was meant to be a challenge to the philosophies of history of the first half of the nineteenth century, particularly to the philosophy of George Friedrich Hegel (1770-1831). Ranke's critical methods were very influential in the practice of history up to the mid-twentieth century, when they were challenged by E.H. Carr. The latter opposed Ranke's ideas of empiricism, arguing 'historians do not merely report facts, rather they choose which facts they use'.

On writing history, contrary to von Ranke's convictions, George Friedrich Hegel (philosopher and historian) advanced three methods or modes of doing history: *original history*, *reflective history* and *philosophical history*. Hegel convincingly explained *original history* by citing the works of Herodotus and Thucydides, that is, writings limited to deeds, events and states of society which they had before their very eyes and whose culture they shared. According to Hegel, *reflective history* is written at some temporal distance from the events or the history considered. However, for Hegel, this form of history has a tendency to impose the cultural prejudices and ideas of the historian's era upon the past history over which the historian reflects. According to Hegel, *philosophical history* is the true way. Hegel maintained that with *philosophical history*, the historian must bracket his own preconceptions and go and find the overall sense and the driving ideas out of the very matter of the history considered. In this case, this book, therefore, has also directly been influenced by Hegelian's *original history* and *reflective history*.

I have to point out one or two things about my selection of the names I have used in this book. First, almost all of them are in Chitumbuka, the dominant language in northern Malawi. Although inhabitants of different districts in northern Malawi speak different languages, for instance, Chitumbuka in Rumphi District, Chitonga in Nkhata-Bay District, Chingoni in parts of Mzimba District and Chinkhonde in Karonga District, Chitumbuka is the dominant language in the region and more of a *lingua franca* at 'regional level'. Since my subjects are labour migrants and traders mainly from the northern region, I settled for Chitumbuka. Second, the names used have meanings which are in line with the dominant theme of the book: the plight or suffering of these traders and labour migrants. The following are some of the names in question: Tiyezge (let us try); Masuzgo (troubles); Tilitose (we are together); Tiwonge (we should be grateful); Tiyenkhu (where should we go? Actually meaning 'what is our last resort?'); Nkhwachi (anyway); Tilipo (we are still around); Vyamucharo (things of this world); Mutende (peace); Panganani (agree on *modus operandi*); Pilirani (persevere); and Tambulani (suffer). Collectively, these names depict hope, suspense and despair on the part of these labour migrants and traders.

Using the Rankean method, I have made efforts to reflect on the experiences of Malawian labour migrants and traders as closely as possible. For labour migrants, their experiences are drawn from both the old period (pre-1990 period) and the new post-1990 period. Contrariwise, the traders' experiences are drawn largely from the new migration period since commercial migration to South Africa is a new phenomenon in Malawi's migration history. In addition, Hegel's *original history* and *reflective history* also come into play throughout the book. This is because I am also writing about the new period during which

I personally share the experiences of these migrants and traders, being one of these migrants ('travellers') myself. Although the majority aboard the coaches between Malawi and South Africa are labour migrants and traders, some are migrants traveling for various other reasons, for example, educational purposes like myself.

In chapter one I provide a succinct account of the history of labour migration from Malawi to South Africa largely during the colonial period (1890s-1964) and post-colonial period (1964 onwards). During the latter, I compare the situation during the reign of Dr. Hastings Kamuzu Banda under the Malawi Congress Party (MCP) (1964-1994) from that during the multi-party or democracy period (1994 onwards). Through such a comparison, I ably show that many Malawian labour migrants, including traders, went to South Africa in the post-1994 period. This was orchestrated by the faltering of Malawi's economy mainly due to mal-administration and corruption tendencies under the successive democratic governments. A good case in point is the heartless privatization of otherwise vibrant state-controlled institutions masterminded by President Bakili Muluzi between 1994 and 2004. It is no mere coincidence, therefore, that this period has been dubbed Malawi's 'lost decade' by academicians and political critics.

In chapters two and three I highlight the plight of labour migrants and traders *en route* between Malawi and South Africa and their desperate attempts to overcome challenges. Chapter two focuses on challenges like incessant demands for *viphuphu* (bribes) by traffic police officers, immigration officers and customs officers. It also touches on unforeseen delays, especially at various border posts, as labour migrants and traders make efforts to 'buy their way'. Chapter three takes a swipe at various types of *viphuphu* involving labour migrants, traders and drivers, on the one hand, and immigration officers, home affairs officials, customs officers and traffic police officers, on the other hand. The chapter shows that labour migrants are largely behind the delays during passport clearance when going to South Africa while traders cause delays when entering Malawi as they try to clear their trade goods.

Chapter five examines the spread of Malawian culture abroad through migration. It argues that though in minority, labour migrants play a central role in spreading various aspects of Malawian culture abroad. The key aspects examined in this chapter are language, dressing, and traditional dances. The various aspects of Malawian culture exported are in line with the major migrating ethnic groups in Malawi, for instance, the Ngoni and the Tumbuka in the northern region, the Chewa in the central region, and the Yao in the southern region. In short, it would be proper to argue that labour migration plays a central role in the popularization of Malawian culture, especially in the southern Africa region.

Chapters four and six examine the challenges that migrants face in South Africa. These include scarcity of jobs, high crime rate, xenophobia, arrests and eventual deportations. On xenophobia, chapter six highlights the failed role of the Malawi government in promoting the welfare of Malawian citizens based in South Africa. Instead of being proactive, the government is largely seen to be reactive in approach: merely coming to the migrants' rescue when irreparable damage has already been done; when labour migrants and traders have lost lives and property following violent attacks on foreigners and looting during waves of xenophobia in South Africa. Instead, the chapter proposes, the government is supposed to root out the actual cause behind the influx of migrants from Malawi to

South Africa over time. In addition, since migration can hardly be stemmed out 'bar and all', the government is supposed to oversee the welfare of its citizens, for instance, by engaging the South African government for special work permits, in line with what other countries in the region are already doing, for example, Zimbabwe.

Harvey C. Chidoba Banda
Mzuzu University, 2017

Chapter One

An Overview of Migration from Malawi

Malawi is one of the countries in southern Africa with a rich and complex migration history. Its long history of migration is a result of its geographical location, natural resources, colonial history and its legacy, among other factors. Malawi is a small land-locked country in south-central Africa bordered by Tanzania to the north and north-east, Zambia to the west, and is almost enveloped on the southern part by Mozambique. The fact that Malawi is land-locked means that it spends a lot of money on importation of manufactured goods, most of which cannot be produced locally. In addition, Malawi is endowed with good natural resources including fertile soils favourable for the cultivation of different types of crops. What is more, the colonial masters concluded, somewhat wrongly though, that Malawi did not have mineral resources, hence the need for its people to focus on the cultivation of crops and rearing of livestock in order to meet their basic subsistence.

Before highlighting developments which inadvertently led to the increase in migration from Malawi, there is need to highlight the history of labour migration from Malawi to other countries, especially to Zimbabwe (then Southern Rhodesia) and South Africa. Broadly, there are two forms of migration: voluntary migration and involuntary migration. On the one hand, under voluntary migration people move out of choice for various reasons, for instance, looking for jobs (labour migration) and for trade purposes (commercial migration). On the other hand, under involuntary migration people are forced to move from their areas of habitual residence due to circumstances beyond their control, for instance, due to wars, earthquakes and floods. In this case, Malawian migrants come under voluntary migration. For a long time Malawians have been going to South Africa and Zimbabwe because of lack of income-earning opportunities within the country.

Malawians have been emigrating to South Africa for wage employment since the late nineteenth century. This development followed the establishment of diamond and gold mines in the Witwatersrand area in South Africa. It is worth noting that diamond was discovered in 1867 while gold was discovered slightly later in 1886. History has it that it was the Tonga from Nkhata-Bay District in northern Malawi that were pioneers in this labour migration. The missionaries established Bandawe Mission at Chintheche in Nkhata-Bay in 1881 and thereafter opened various schools. After attaining basic education from these schools, the Tonga started looking for jobs. Initially they sought jobs from the Shire Highlands area in Blantyre in southern Malawi before the same missionaries alerted them about the existence of better-paying jobs in the South African mines. This marked the beginning of a century-old history of labour migration to the mines.

The history of labour migration from Malawi to South Africa can be categorized into two clear-cut periods: the old migration period and the new migration period. The old migration period existed between the 1880s and 1980s. During this period, labour migration took two forms: formal or contract migration and informal migration, locally referred to as *selufu* (from self-migration). While *selufu* existed throughout the old migration period, formal migration only took place from 1903 onwards. The South African Chamber of Mines, a body responsible for mine management, established agencies to mastermind the process of labour recruitment on its behalf.

The Native Recruitment Corporation (NRC) was in charge over local labour recruitment whereas the Witwatersrand Native Labour Association (WNLA) popularly known as *Wenela* recruited foreign labour from countries as far as Malawi (then Nyasaland).

From 1903 onwards formal labour migrants were recruited by *Wenela*. However, formal recruitment was intermittent unlike informal migration (*selufu*) which tended to occur throughout. For instance, between 1909 and 1934 formal recruitment was banned because of high mortality rate among mine workers. The tropical workers who included Malawian labour migrants were not used to the cold weather and suffered from pneumonia. In addition, they also suffered from tuberculosis due to unhealthy living conditions in the mine compounds. *Wenela* resumed its recruitment activities in Nyasaland in 1935. It is worth noting that labour migrants continued to go to South Africa during the ban years under *selufu*.

By 1940 the Rhodesia Native Labour Bureau (RNLB), locally called *Mthandizi* which means helper, joined the labour migration scene in Nyasaland and started recruiting labour for the Southern Rhodesian farms. Eventually, this brought about fierce competition for Malawian labour between *Wenela* and *Mthandizi*. *Wenela* established recruitment stations in selected districts across the country. Some of these stations were established in districts such as Mzimba (northern Malawi), Dowa, Dezda and Ntcheu (central Malawi) and Blantyre and Mangochi (southern Malawi). Later on, *Mthandizi* also established its own recruitment stations close to those of *Wenela*. Each of the two recruiting agencies devised strategies to attract as many migrants as possible. For instance, *Wenela* provided transport, food and accommodation and also offered higher wages. Not ready to be outsmarted by *Wenela*, *Mthandizi* allowed its labour recruits to emigrate together with their wives plus at least a child. This arrangement of family migration proved attractive to some Malawians. In addition, farm work proved to be less arduous than mine work, hence more attractive. It is partly because of this reason that some of the wives ended up being engaged to do some farm activities like weeding. However, overall it was *Wenela* which was more attractive to potential Malawian migrants. Malawian labour migrants eventually exercised choice either to emigrate under *Wenela*, *Mthandizi* or *selufu*.

Wenela's recruitment operations came to an end in 1974 following the plane crash in Francistown in Botswana which killed 74 Malawian migrants. These labour migrants were *en route* to Malawi at the end of their mine contracts. Following this incident Dr. Banda banned all recruitment operations by *Wenela*. He was in favour of Malawians providing labour locally, especially on the newly-established tobacco estates. However, two years later (1976) Malawi re-negotiated with the Chamber of Mines for the resumption of labour recruitment activities in Malawi. The government had realized that Malawi's economy continuously needed the foreign income through the export of labour to the mines. Consequently, recruitment resumed in 1977 under the auspices of The Employment Bureau of Africa (TEBA), popularly known as *Theba*. However, *Theba* started recruiting small numbers of Malawians as compared to its predecessor, *Wenela*. This was partly a result of the policy of internalization (also called stabilization) and mechanization espoused by the Chamber of Mines in the 1970s. This policy was aimed at cutting down on the recruitment costs by the mines. As a result of this, the majority of potential Malawian migrants were not recruited and opted for *selufu* instead.

Theba's recruitment operations lasted for ten years when in 1987 they came to an abrupt end as a result of the dispute between Malawi and South Africa over HIV testing. South Africa requested Malawi to allow its recruits to be screened for HIV that causes AIDS. Malawi did not agree with this condition, arguing HIV testing was supposed to be a voluntary, and not a compulsory, undertaking in line with the principles of the World Health Organization (WHO). Malawi further wondered why this compulsory HIV testing was to apply only to Malawi and not to other labour source countries in the southern Africa region like Botswana. Consequently, *Theba* stopped recruiting labour in Malawi in 1988 and between 1988 and 1992 South Africa repatriated all Malawian labour migrants from the South African mines.

The new migration period can be traced from the early 1990s onwards. The decline in mine migrancy led to the increase in *selufu*. Since *Theba* stopped recruiting labour for the mines, all migrants emigrated informally to South Africa. Informal migration also increased following the collapse of apartheid and the introduction of democratic governance in 1994. This development also led to the influx of immigrants into South Africa from other countries. In Malawi the transition from one party to multi-party politics also facilitated the increase in informal labour migration. There was also improvement in the mode of transport, especially with the introduction of coaches between the two countries. Within a short period of time, local transporters also joined the migration scene. Gradually even women started emigrating to South Africa, initially accompanying husbands but later even as single migrants. This time migrants were no longer destined to the mines, but rather to various work places in the informal sector.

The sections that follow highlight the declining trend over the years in the fields of manufacturing, mining, agriculture and fishing and how this trend inadvertently led to the increasing need for the affected Malawians to resort to emigration not only for wage employment, but also for commercial purposes.

Agro-based Economy

Malawi's economy is based on agriculture. For many years during both the colonial and post-colonial period, at least up to the end 1980s, Malawi had a thriving agriculture industry. During this period, Malawi's economy relied on tea plantations, especially in the Shire Highlands in the southern region. Following the attainment of independence, Dr. Banda encouraged the opening of tobacco estates in the fertile plains in central and northern Malawi. Although this initiative eventually bore fruit, a cross-section of Malawians in selected migration areas in the country continued to rely on emigration for wage employment in the mines in South Africa. With time, tobacco, tea and coffee became the main sources of foreign exchange revenue. Of these, it was tobacco, dubbed Malawi's 'green gold', which topped the list in terms of foreign exchange value. Consequently, more and more Malawians resorted to tobacco cultivation as their main cash crop. Dr. Banda encouraged Malawians to grow more and good quality tobacco, arguing *chuma chili mdongo* (wealth is in the soil).

Malawians eventually developed the habit of investing in tobacco production. Even labour migrants returning from wage employment in South Africa, Zambia and Zimbabwe invested their proceeds in cash crop farming, mainly in tobacco. Although for many years tobacco was behind the enrichment of several households in the country, gradually soils started losing fertility. As a result, tobacco farmers started operating on losses. Despite this, because of the entrenched mentality that tobacco is a source of wealth, many Malawians continued with tobacco cultivation. The declining soil fertility went hand in hand with the increasing prices of fertilizer following the weakening of the Malawi Kwacha against the major international currencies like the British Pound, the South African Rand and the United States Dollar. The Malawi Kwacha persevered against these currencies for many years between 1964 and 1994. For instance, in the period up to the 1970s, the Kwacha traded favourably with both the Rand and the Pound.

Tobacco production was behind the notable infrastructural development in most of the tobacco growing areas in Malawi. Central region districts like Kasungu and Lilongwe experienced notable economic growth during the one party regime under Dr. Banda between 1964 and 1994. This growth was attributed to large-scale tobacco production. The same applied to the northern region districts of Rumphi and Mzimba. The majority of tobacco farmers in these districts amassed a lot of wealth and as a result embarked on massive infrastructural development projects like houses and buildings for shops and renting purposes. These farmers also embarked on transport businesses by buying mini-buses and lorries for hire. In the process, they were able to provide employment to fellow Malawians at societal and district level. Examples of such big tobacco farmers in Rumphi District included Mr. Mkanadothi Kumwenda, Mr. Gotani Mkandawire, Mr. Mtimbura Luhanga and Mr. Yagontha Mnthali. With time these farmers diversified their investments into transport business, buying a fleet of heavy-duty trucks in the process.

It is interesting to note that the peak of tobacco production in the northern region was responsible for the mass migration of *matenanti* (tenant farmers) from the southern region to tobacco estates in Rumphi District. Growing up at Rumphi *boma* in the 1980s and early 1990s, I personally witnessed this kind of internal migration. In August and September every year, lorries full of *matenanti* poured into the district, returning with these farmers in June after tobacco sales the following year. However, this tenant system was exploitative in that *matenanti* relied on *katapila* (loans with fifty or one hundred per cent interest repayment rate) from their employers. For instance, they used to get foodstuffs like maize and beans for their daily subsistence on such credit. Hence *matenanti* were liable to hefty deductions after tobacco sales by way of paying back these huge loans. In most cases, most of these *matenanti* made meagre yearly profits from their tobacco farming. It was also not uncommon to find some *matenanti* operating on a virtual loss. Consequently, this system ushered in a vicious cycle whereby *matenanti* could only make ends meet by renegotiating such contract farming with their employers. As a result of the entrenchment of this exploitative system, which was more similar to, than different from, the *thangata* system of the earlier colonial period in Malawi, a good number of Malawians had no intention whatsoever to emigrate to South Africa for wage employment.

In a twist to the tale, although tobacco was the main foreign exchange earner for many years since independence in 1964, the situation changed following the anti-tobacco campaigns and the consequent collapse of prices on the international market from the 1990s onwards. Consequently, tobacco farmers started experiencing the pinch by getting low rewards from their tobacco sales. Despite this and mainly because of the entrenched mindset that wealth generation is mainly through tobacco, farmers continued growing tobacco, deemed Malawi's 'green gold'. Consequently, year in year out farmers continued operating on losses. The impact was even more pronounced on *matenanti*. Most of them virtually became destitute, even failing to make annual trips to their home villages after tobacco harvest and sales.

From the 2000s onwards, the impact was so grave that both the government and various Non-Governmental Organizations (NGOs) intervened in the matter. They launched a nation-wide campaign which was aimed at urging tobacco farmers to embark on diversification in their cash crop production: to stop over-relying on tobacco production, but rather to scale down on tobacco production and at the same time embark on the growing of other alternative cash crops like soya beans and paprika. This campaign had mixed results. While some farmers heeded this call, others stuck to tobacco farming. As a result, the proceeds from tobacco kept on swinging back and forth like a pendulum: in some years tobacco prices were better and farmers went home smiling, and yet in other years the opposite was true, with some farmers even failing to settle their fertilizer loans. On the whole, however, the downward trend in the prices of tobacco continued unabated. By 2005 a significant proportion of these tobacco farmers threw in the towel in as far as tobacco farming was concerned. It is some of these farmers who resorted to growing such crops as beans and paprika. The prices of the latter were enticing for the few formative years before they too became poor. This was partly a result of over-production, hence large supply, which overtook demand, was responsible for poor prices.

In addition to tobacco, Malawians in the past took cultivation of other cash crops seriously. For instance, such cash crops like cotton, tea, coffee and groundnuts fetched a lot of money on the market. Farmers growing cotton, for instance, invested their energies and money in cotton bearing in mind that there was a ready market after harvest. David Whitehead and Sons Limited used to buy this cotton at good prices from these farmers. Unlike during the post-1994 period when this company and other companies were sold in line with privatization, cotton was previously used locally to manufacture cotton products like shirts, pairs of trousers and *vitenje* (wrappers). After 1994 the company was privatized and was later bought by Malawians of Indian origin and became Mapeto Wholesalers.

Under the new management, the cotton company offered poor cotton prices to farmers, arguing this was a result of plummeting cotton prices on the international market. Consequently, most cotton farmers became disillusioned and scaled down on cotton production. This meant a drastic reduction in the number of *maganyu* (piece jobs) on cotton farms. Since this development coincided with the loss of value of tobacco on the market, the resultant impact on employment in the rural areas was quite remarkable and enormous. This trend continued with cotton fetching ever-decreasing prices on the market over the years. Mapeto Wholesalers is no longer a big cotton buyer as compared to David Whitehead in the past. In addition, the influx of other manufactured goods into the country has had a stifling effect on the vibrancy of Mapeto. Consequently, a number of cotton farmers were eventually compelled to virtually dump cotton farming, arguing 'it is a waste of their precious time, energy and resources'. Over the past few years cotton farmers in different parts of the country actually rallied together and organized nation-wide demonstrations against low cotton prices.

Apart from the growing of cash crops, Malawians have been growing various types of food crops since time immemorial. In fact, crops like maize, beans and sweet potatoes do well in alluvial soils found in most parts of the country. Rice is grown in selected parts, especially in the lakeshore districts of Karonga, Nkhata-Bay and Nkhota-Kota. Maize is grown by most households because it is Malawi's staple food crop. What is more, most low lying areas (*dambos*) are suitable for growing different types of vegetables including tomatoes and cabbages. Some places like Jenda in Mzimba District have developed into Rural Growth Centres (RGCs) as a result of farm produce like tomatoes, cabbages, Irish potatoes and different types of vegetables. However, some people still do not benefit much from such farming due to inadequate capital, for instance, for farm input such as fertilizer and pesticides.

Following the attainment of independence in 1964 Malawi established agriculture offices across the country. The officers in these offices supervised proper crop cultivation methods and animal husbandry practices with the aim of ensuring that households achieved food self-sufficiency. The Ministry of Agriculture also posted agriculture extension officers and agriculture assistants in the countryside who worked hand in hand with commercial and subsistence farmers. There was also the famers' clubs where farmers met on a regular basis to brainstorm on the challenges they faced and chart the way forward. With this farming system in place, most farmers benefited from their crop cultivation and animal husbandry. It was, therefore, easy for them to pay back loans of the various farm inputs. This farming system was complemented by the vibrant market which readily bought various farm produce. The government established the Agricultural Development and Marketing Corporation (ADMARC) which had outlets in almost every corner of the country. Even in the rural areas people easily sold their farm produce through ADMARC. What is more, with the system of the government's agricultural subsidy, ADMARC usually bought these farm produce at good prices.

However, this farming and marketing system virtually collapsed with the introduction of the democratic governance in 1994. The government abandoned the system of agriculture assistants, extension workers and farmers' clubs. The new democratically-elected government of the United Democratic Front (UDF) under Bakili Muluzi was bent on reversing the otherwise good policies put in place by the Malawi Congress Party (MCP). As a result, the once-vibrant agricultural production collapsed. This was worsened by the collapse of tobacco prices on the international market following the anti-tobacco campaigns. In addition, people misinterpreted freedoms and threw their hard working spirit to the dogs. In a bid to win elections which came after every five years, the UDF government put in place the system of giving food handouts which in the long run exacerbated laziness on the part of the populace. These are the same people who used to be very hard working during the reign of Dr. Banda between 1964 and 1994.

Although ADMARC continued its operations beyond 1994, its vibrancy is no longer felt on the ground. The government farm subsidy which was responsible for controlling commodity prices in ADMARC depots is no longer there. Consequently, ADMARC continues to buy maize and other farm produce at very low prices and yet offers the same produce at high retail prices. This trend implies farmers selling their produce at a loss and buying the same produce at exorbitant prices thereafter. This has had a negative impact on the living standards and the buying power or Malawians. As a way out, most Malawians shun ADMARC services and instead prefer selling and buying farm produce from *mavenda* (vendors). The latter have actually cashed in on the gap created by ADMARC. *Mavenda* are able to buy farm produce at better prices from farmers and thereafter sell the same to countries like Zambia and Tanzania at better prices, in the process making huge profits. The government has a weak policing mechanism and has, therefore, failed to control the business activities of *mavenda*. In addition, the same *mavenda* are somewhat influential during political campaigns (every five years since 1994), hence remain 'untouchable' if politicians' interest is to retain, and continue with, their political positions.

Malawian farmers also rely on the rearing of various livestock like cattle, sheep, pigs and goats. The majority of households are patrilineal with the man as the head of the household. It is these households which take cattle keeping so seriously that it is the intention of every household to own cattle. Part of this cattle is used to settle *malobolo* (bride price) when sons are getting married. A household with daughters is considered to be wealthy *de jure* since the parents receive cattle from the men's parents when their daughters are getting married. With this arrangement in place, most households in the rural areas had *vibaya* (kraals) full of cattle. However, with time *malobolo* became monetized so that, instead of cattle, money could as well be used as bride price. Together with the ever-increasing prices of cattle, cattle herds started dwindling so that by the 1990s only pockets of households in the countryside still owned large numbers of cattle. There has also been notable changes in the reasons why members of these patriarchal households embark on labour migration journeys to South Africa: in the past they largely emigrated to accumulate money with which to buy cattle, but nowadays they use proceeds from working abroad in making investments in farming, generally, for instance, buying of fertilizer, and in small-scale businesses in the trading centres sprouting in the rural areas.

Mining Industry

Unlike the other former colonial territories like Southern Rhodesia (Zimbabwe) and Northern Rhodesia (Zambia), which had mineral deposits like copper, Malawi (formerly Nyasaland) did not have huge (exploitable) mineral deposits. The only exploitable minerals were coal deposits which housed Kaziwiziwi Coal Mine and, after it's defunct, Mchenga Coal Mine in Rumphi District in northern Malawi. It is interesting to note that during the post-1994 period other mineral explorations led to the mining of uranium at Kayerekera in Karonga District, northern Malawi, and also to the continued exploration of other minerals in various parts of the country. A question one can ask here is 'why should minerals be discovered forty years after the attainment of independence in a country deemed to be without minerals by earlier mineral explorers?' To a lay man, this borders on deceit and incompetence by the so-called earlier crop of explorers.

Although coal had been mined for so many years at Kaziwiziwi Coal Mine and later at Mchenga Coal Mine, it did not bolster Malawi's economy since it is less profitable when compared to such minerals as gold and diamond. These latter two minerals were not discovered in Malawi. As a result, for a long time, coal merely supported various manufacturing industries which were mainly housed in the cities of Lilongwe and Blantyre. Mzuzu which was established as a city in northern Malawi in the 1980s, has largely been neglected by the successive governments so that it hardly boasts of major manufacturing industries. A few of the latter only got established in Mzuzu around the 2000s. This means that coal is transported over huge distances from Rumphi District in northern Malawi to where it is finally used in Lilongwe and Blantyre in central region and southern region, respectively, hence huge production and general operation costs. Zomba which was elevated to the status of a city in the post-1994 period, is mainly an academic town housing several secondary schools, Domasi College of Education which is a secondary school teacher training college under the Ministry of Education and Chancellor College, a main constituent college of the University of Malawi.

The establishment of a uranium mine at Kayerekera in Karonga brought about hopes in the minds of many Malawians that it will end up bolstering the economy since uranium fetches higher prices on the market as compared to coal and other minerals. This was in addition to hopes of creating a number of jobs for a cross-section of Malawians, especially those semi-skilled job seekers in the northern districts of Karonga, Chitipa and Rumphi. In fact, some labour migration specialists thought that in the long run Kayerekera Uranium Mine had the potential of absorbing the former *Wenela* and *Theba* mine migrant workers who stopped working in South African mines following the decline and eventual collapse in mine migrancy in the 1970s and 1980s, respectively.

However, in practice what actually happened was actually the opposite. With the inception of corrupt practices from 1994 onwards by the various successive democratic governments, mining at Kayerekera was hugely affected by corruption. Paladin Africa in charge of mining uranium at Kayerekera, was, reportedly, remitting very little money to the government. A lot of money ended up in the pockets of greedy politicians so much so that the government and Malawians at large benefited little from the uranium proceeds. Even in terms of employment, there was ineffective supervision by the relevant government's mining ministry and departments. As a result, not many people secured jobs at the mine. It is not surprising, therefore, that Kayerekera Uranium Mine in Karonga had little impact in reducing the numbers of Malawians emigrating for wage employment abroad. This scenario continued until the mine was finally closed due to a wrangle between the government and Paladin Africa over mining proceeds and also due to huge operation costs.

Contrary to peoples' expectations in Karonga District and Malawi as a whole, uranium mining at Kayerekera brought more misery than goodness to the district. The mine was responsible for the skyrocketing of prices of most commodities and services in the district. Food prices, for example, in the restaurants and bars went up by almost one hundred per cent. The same applied to prices of hotels, lodges and rest-houses in Karonga District and the surrounding areas. Within a few years after the establishment of the mine, the cost of living in the district soared. In general, the life of the people in areas surrounding the mine also worsened. Despite many complaints from the society, Kayerekera Mine did little to uplift the living standards of the communities. It is not surprising to note that the mine was closed amidst allegations of rampant corrupt practices by both government and mine officials. All the hopes that people had about the potentiality of the uranium mine came to a grinding halt.

Manufacturing Industry

Malawi's manufacturing industry has shrunk over the years, the situation worsening following the transition from one-party regime under the once-mighty Malawi Congress Party (MCP) to multi-party politics in 1994. From the attainment of independence in 1964, the then president, Dr. Hastings Kamuzu Banda, maintained friendly ties with Britain, Malawi's former colonial master. In so doing and with the continued financial support, Malawi was able to woo investors into the country. Consequently, its manufacturing base grew steadily with time. It is not surprising, therefore, that between 1964 and 1994 Malawi boasted of such manufacturing companies as Brown and Clapperton (B&C), Mandala Motors, David Whitehead and Sons Limited, and Southern Bottlers (SOBO). Through the local manufacturing of clothes, drinks and the processing of farm produce, Malawi was able to create the much-needed employment for its citizenry. Through this employment, coupled with the availability of employment in the civil service, a cross-section of Malawians were able to cater for the needs of their households locally, that is, without the need to emigrate abroad.

This does not mean that the phenomenon of migration was non-existent. Malawians used to emigrate largely for wage employment, albeit on a smaller scale. In fact, a large proportion of this migration was controlled by the interstate agreement between the governments of Malawi and South Africa. Through the system of quotas, a fixed number of migrants emigrated either under *Wenela* or *Theba*, afterwards. Although a cross-section of Malawians emigrated informally under *selufu*, the numbers were relatively small. This was partly a result of the fact that women were not officially allowed to emigrate. Relatively fewer numbers of women also emigrated informally partly due to the numerous challenges associated with *selufu*: initially *selufu* migrants literally travelled on foot, in the process facing all kinds of challenges *en route* to South Africa. In fact, some of them never reached their ultimate destination, South Africa – they were killed by dangerous wild animals and sometimes died of 'incurable' diseases.

Since 1994 and especially following the massive and careless privatization of state-controlled companies, most of the manufacturing companies ended up ceasing their operations. These included Brown and Clapperton and Mandala Motors and Grain and Milling Company Limited, among others. This development had a deleterious effect on the already fragile economy. Consequently employment opportunities became even scarcer. Most of the available employment opportunities were low paying and this is partly the reason why a cross-section of unskilled and semi-skilled Malawians had the tendency of opting to emigrate for wage employment abroad. Most of these people preferred to work in South Africa's relatively buoyant informal sector.

Companies under the once-vibrant Press Corporation Limited (PCL) such as Press Bakeries Limited also felt the privatization pinch. They ended up being sold and in their stead a host of subsidiary companies emerged. This development came hand in hand with the lowering of the quality of their products. This was in stark contrast to the pre-1990 period when quality was at the heart of almost each and every company. Largely due to general mismanagement and corruption tendencies, their production capacities, and consequently profit margins, collapsed. No wonder in order to remain buoyant, they resorted to massive retrenchments on a regular basis.

Equally companies like Grain and Milling Company Limited were eventually liquidated. This was a blow in a country whose staple food for the majority of households is *sima* made of maize flour. Grain and Milling Company was replaced by Rab Processors Limited, a company owned by Malawians of Asian origin. However, comparatively the prices and quality of flour products by Rab Processors paled in the face of products from the defunct Grain and Milling Company Limited. Although Malawians also rely on meals from *mpunga* (rice) and *mbambayira* (Irish potatoes), these two farm produce are generally regarded as expensive for the average Malawi household. Put differently, the majority of Malawians can hardly afford meals from *mpunga* and *mbambayira* on a regular basis. Stories are told of children from ordinary households who complain of sleeping on empty stomachs after eating rice and Irish potatoes as part of their supper as long as they have not eaten *sima*. The increasing maize flour prices, therefore, continues to haunt Malawian parents in their quest of fending for their households.

With the declining soil fertility and the consequent drop in maize production, efforts were made by the government and Non-Governmental Organizations to encourage Malawians to diversify their food choices. They were encouraged to rely on the cultivation of food crops which do not require input like fertilizer. This was a result of the realization that it was extremely expensive to produce maize because of ever-increasing fertilizer prices. On the diversification agenda were such food crops like sweet potatoes, cassava, Irish potatoes and various types of vegetables including beans. Similarly, Malawians were encouraged to diversify on their relish dishes since there was a declining trend in the rearing of livestock like cattle, goats and sheep. Instead they were encouraged to grow more leguminous plants like beans which did not require fertilizer during cultivation. However, because of the entrenched and deep-seated mindset, that is, the firm belief that *sima* is the only reliable meal, the response to such calls for diversification was but gradual and minimal. This scenario has continued beyond the year 2000.

Fishing Industry

Malawi is endowed with Lake Malawi which is home for more than five hundred species of fish. This is a clear water lake and is the third largest lake in Africa. This lake has a great economic potential as its different types of fish, for example, the *chambo* and *mpasa*, are an attraction not only to Malawians, but also to people from abroad. Consequently, there is a vibrant fishing business in fresh and sun-dried fish across the country. People from the lakeshore districts of Karonga, Rumphi, Nkhata-Bay, Salima and Mangochi rely on fish sales to realize money for their daily subsistence. They use money realised from fish sales to meet their daily needs including payment of school fees and buying farm input. However, since they have to buy fishing gear, the increasing prices of such equipment compel some fishermen to emigrate to countries like Tanzania where they buy cheap fishing equipment like nets. With time, there developed a practice of these people seeking wage employment in Tanzania and thereafter using proceeds to buy fishing equipment. This practice has grown in the recent years, especially in Nkhata-Bay District in northern Malawi.

Apart from Lake Malawi, there are other smaller lakes like Lake Malombe, Lake Chilwa and Lake Kazuni which are equally reliable sources of different types of fish. There are also big perennial rivers like Bua, Limphasa, North Rukuru and South Rukuru and Shire which are also sources of fish. Despite these various fish sources, fish remains expensive, especially when transported to up-lying and mountainous areas in different parts of the country. Consequently, it is only the well-to-do Malawians that afford fish as relish in their meals on a regular basis. As for the ordinary Malawians, fish relish remains 'a luxury', something they can merely afford during special occasions like weddings, parties and the festive seasons like Christmas.

It was partly a result of the declining trend in the above sectors which weakened Malawi's economy, in the process leading to acute unemployment problems. Consequently, by the early 1990s large numbers of Malawians, especially from the major migration areas, opted to emigrate to such countries as South Africa, Tanzania and Zimbabwe either for wage employment or for business purposes. Chapter two highlights some of the challenges that the labour migrants and traders face *en route* to and from South Africa, while chapter four highlights some of the challenges that they face during their stay in South Africa. In general, traders stay briefly, for instance, from a few days to a few weeks while labour migrants usually stay longer since they go to South Africa to work. These labour migrants stay briefly in Malawi during holiday because they have to go back to South Africa and resume work otherwise they risk losing their jobs to other job seekers.

Photograph 1: A compound owned by a Malawian *mtchona* (overstayer) in Diepsloot, Johannesburg. He went to South Africa in the 1950s and worked in the mines up to the 1970s. From the 1980s he secured a different job till he retired around 2000s. Thereafter, he invested part of his proceeds in rented apartments. However, he indicated he still maintained contacts with his home people, visiting them once every two years (photo by author).

Chapter Two

Of Migrants' Journeys: Traders' and Labour Migrants' Experiences

Labour migrants and traders face all kinds of challenges on their way to and from South Africa. While the challenges faced by traders are more contemporary since commercial migration is traced to as far back as the early 1990s, labour migrants challenges date back to the inception of labour migration from Malawi to South Africa in the last part of the nineteenth century. In fact, during the old migration period, that is, between the 1880s and 1980s *selufu* labour migrants faced more challenges as compared to formal or recruited migrants. The latter travelled without any hurdles since everything was arranged and provided for by the recruiting organisations. *Selufu* migrants, on the other hand, organized their own means of travel with some actually traveling on foot during the early years. During the contemporary period, however, these labour migrants face new kinds of challenges altogether. These challenges mostly have to do with traveling using invalid documentation including expired visas. However, this problem does not seriously affect traders since they do not stay long in South Africa: they return to Malawi before the expiry of their 30-day visas.

Labour Migrants' Experiences during the Old Period

During the old period Malawians were emigrating to Zambia, Tanzania, Zimbabwe and South Africa to look for jobs. Most of the latter were found in the mines, with a few jobs found in the other sectors like agriculture and construction. For many years these labour migrants were emigrating informally, that is, under *selufu*. This was especially the case before the introduction of labour recruiting organizations like *Wenela*, *Mthandizi* and *Theba*. In Zambia these migrants were working in the copper mines on the copperbelt. In Zimbabwe the majority of these labour migrants worked on the farms, while in South Africa migrants were mainly attracted to the gold and diamond mines. Even after the beginning of formal labour recruitment, these migrants exercised choice either to emigrate under *selufu* or under the various recruiting organizations.

Since the beginning of labour migration to South Africa all the way up to the 1950s, labour migrants were virtually walking on foot to their respective destination countries. This was before the introduction of lorry transport and railways. Consequently, the trips to South Africa were very dangerous and tiresome. There are stories of migrants sometimes being attacked by dangerous wild animals along the way. Some of them actually lost their lives. Upon being attacked, those who were lucky to escape alive proceeded with their journeys while their friends were devoured by hungry lions. A story is told of some Malawian migrants who stumbled on fresh meat and their first impression was that it was meat from a wild animal dropped by, say, a lion. A few metres from this scene then they found a head of a human being! At this point they then concluded that the meat they had found previously was actually of a dead person killed and devoured by beasts! At first they had intentions of eating this meat and they could have eaten human meat.

Selufu migrants also faced food challenges along the way. Although they used to carry food starter packs like *vimphonde* made of roast groundnuts, these could not suffice because migrants spent many days before reaching their destinations. Once their prepared foodstuffs were depleted, problems set in. At this point, they ate almost anything that was edible just to ensure basic survival. At this point, migrants maintain, they were not very different from wild animals. They could not choose what to eat. Some of them were collapsing of acute hunger. One migrant had this to say on this: *'Pala munyithu wafwa munthowa, tikamubikanga ndipo paumaliro ise tikalutiliranga na ulendo withu'*. (If one of us died, we used to bury the dead body and thereafter we were proceeding with our journey). While on the way, they could branch and ask for food assistance from nearby villages. But at the same time, they had to tread carefully not to come into contact with authorities like the police to avoid capture.

As part of their efforts to reach their destination, they had to overcome these food problems. Hence they were at times having stoppages along the way. They could camp in an area for some weeks or even months. They were looking for *maganyu* (piece jobs) in order to find food. After accumulating enough, they proceeded with their journey to South Africa. In some cases, it so happened that they got preoccupied with *maganyu* along the way, staying longer in an area than they anticipated. In some cases, this place eventually turned out to be their ultimate destination *de facto*. After working and accumulating some proceeds, they returned to Malawi and never reached South Africa. In this connection, a significant proportion of these labour migrants destined for the South African mines ended up working in Zimbabwe and Zambia.

Bearing in mind that they were making a journey into an unknown world, labour migrants made efforts to prepare adequately for this journey. In addition to carrying some foodstuffs, they also carried *mankhwala* (medicine) in powder form with which to treat diseases in case they fell sick. However, they could only prepare medicine for common diseases. While on the way, some migrants fell sick and in some cases the strange disease could not be treated by the medicine they carried. Tiyezge had this to say on this matter: *'Nyengo zinyake munthowa tikaluwalanga matenda ghachilendo, apa vikatisuzganga chifukwa mankhwala agho tikayeghanga ghakatondekanga kuchizga matenda ghachilendo aghá*. (Sometimes we suffered from some strange disease and in this case we had problems since the medicine we carried proved ineffective). They were lucky if this happened close to a residential area, in which case they sought assistance from the people in the area or from a nearby hospital, if there was one. But some migrants maintained that in rare cases some migrants ended up dying of these diseases, despite efforts to cure the disease.

Migrants faced the greatest challenges in trying to cross from Zimbabwe into South Africa, the dream land or the land of unlimited opportunities. The South Africa border was policed and most sections heavily and jealously guarded. All those migrants captured by the authorities upon entry were declared prisoners and were taken to a notorious farm prison at Bethal. Here captives were kept under quarantine for about six months. During this period, they were serving their sentence of illegal entry into South Africa. Oral tradition among former *selufu* migrants in Malawi has a rich heritage of their experiences on this farm. The farm prison is locally referred to as *Bethani* and the collection of stories, the *Bethani* stories. One former *selufu* migrant had this to say on his experience at *Bethani*:

Apo tikafumanga mu Zimbabwe kunjira mu South Africa bapolisi bakatikora ndipo bakatilutiska ku Bethani. Agha ghakaba malo apo bose abo bakoreka bakabajaliranga. Tikakhala myezi sikisi ndipo nyengo yose iyi tikajimanga mbambayira na mawoko. Pa umaliro bakatileka ndipo bakati tili banangwa kupenja ntchito mu South Africa.

(When we were leaving Zimbabwe and we wanted to enter South Africa, we were captured by the authorities and sent to Bethal farm prison. Here we stayed for six months. During all this period we were forced to dig Irish potatoes using our bare hands. At the end, we were released, telling us we were now free to look for employment in South Africa.)

It is maintained that the prison graduates were even being given a kind of certificate that they had served their sentence at Bethal. This document also assisted these *selufu* migrants to secure employment in towns. Most of these *selufu* migrants ended up becoming *matchona* (the overstayers) in South Africa.

From the 1950s it was relatively easier for *selufu* migrants to travel to South Africa. This was a result of the introduction of lorry transport, especially between Nyasaland (Malawi) and Southern Rhodesia (Zimbabwe). This transport, known as *ulere* (literally meaning free service), was introduced by *Mthandizi* which recruited labour for the Zimbabwean farms. Some migrants would be transported to Zimbabwe using this transport, only to abandon the farm jobs in Zimbabwe and embark on a journey to South Africa to work either in the mines or in other sectors. Others used railway transport to the Zambian copper-belt where they largely worked in the copper mines.

Unlike *selufu* migrants who were facing numerous challenges on their way to South Africa, formal labour migrants, initially under *Wenela* and later under *Theba*, were experiencing stress-free journeys to South Africa. The recruiting organisations were providing everything starting with transport, food and even accommodation upon arrival in

South Africa. The only problem they faced had to do with ensuring that they were recruited since the recruitment process was rigorous. They were subjected to a tough screening process. Only healthy and physically strong young men were recruited. All the weaklings were left out. It is indicated that those physically weak, but healthy men were stall fed for about two weeks to ensure they gained weight. After this period, their weights were checked once more and only those who had gained some weight were engaged. This was done in view of the rigorous nature of mine work. The latter was physically debilitating, hence only suitable for the physically strong and healthy men. This is what one migrant said on the toughness of getting recruited in a district without a recruitment station:

Our friends from Mzimba District had the advantage of being close to *Wenela* recruiting station, hence could easily get engaged. As for us, there was no station in Nkhata-Bay that's why most of us ended up emigrating under *selufu*. This was in spite of the numerous challenges associated with emigrating informally. Those who were determined to still emigrate under *Wenela*, they travelled all the way from Nkhata-Bay to Mzimba to get recruited.

This view was supported by a number of migrants from Nkhata-Bay District. In fact, even former labour migrants from Mzimba District shared the same view. They maintained that it was easier and straight forward to get engaged by *Wenela* and later by *Theba* in Mzimba District. The same applied to other districts in the country in which *Wenela* established their recruitment stations.

The majority of labour migrants in Mzimba District and other districts with recruitment centres in Malawi emigrating through formal means, that is, by getting engaged by *Wenela* and later *Theba*. This was largely a result of the easiness of getting to South Africa since transport and meals were provided to recruits. Comparatively, those who emigrated under *selufu* suffered *en route* to South Africa. Those who went under *selufu* did so as a last resort after being turned back by *Wenela* and *Theba*. Even fewer migrants actually chose to voluntarily emigrate under *selufu*, arguing it was flexible for them to change employers in South Africa since they were not bound by fixed contracts under *Wenela* and *Theba*.

Since it was difficult to get recruited by these recruiting agencies, there are stories of a few potential labour migrants who resorted to the use of *mankhwala gha chifipa* (local medicine) in order to boost their chances of getting recruited. In this case, they approached herbalists for such *mankhwala* (medicine). But after getting recruited, formal migrants never faced any hurdles along the way. They narrated that they largely used road and railway transport to South Africa, They either went through Mozambique or Zimbabwe before reaching their final destination, South Africa.

However, after some time *Wenela* introduced flights between Malawi and South Africa usually going through Botswana. With time transporting labour migrants between Malawi and South Africa proved to be a costly and hardly sustainable venture, and this was partly the reason why the Chamber of Mines eventually thought of embarking on a process of localization or stabilization and mechanization. Under very rare circumstances, labour migrants faced the problem of accidents. A good example here is the 1974 plane crash accident on the way to Malawi at Francistown in Botswana. Such accidents, though rare, were behind the decision by the Malawi government to ban recruitment activities by *Wenela* in Malawi in 1974.

Labour Migrants' Experiences during the New Period

Compared with the old period, that is, the pre-1990 period, labour migrants and traders face more problems when traveling between Malawi and South Africa during the new period, that is, during the post-1990 period. These problems were more pronounced in the early 1990s when transporters had just started plying their business between Malawi and South Africa. Initially, it was a few coaches transporting people and *katundu* (goods) before local transports joined the transport scene. Again, at first the local transporters were of South African origin, with Malawians simply playing the role of transport assistants. However, gradually these Malawians learnt the business and slowly joined the scene. Though inexperienced, Malawian local transporters easily gained the confidence of fellow Malawians wanting to travel to South Africa and back to Malawi. Comparatively, a good number of South African transporters gained the reputation of being crooked and duping potential migrants. They would collect transport money in advance and either fail to start off on the appointed day or start off without actually carrying passengers. The latter option was so common since they could collect money from more people way beyond the capacity of their type of transport, for example, a seven-tonne lorry.

Despite the advantages of trustworthiness, Malawian local transporters had the problem of financial capacity. They usually did not have adequate capital outlay to run their transport business. They had a lorry or a mini-bus quite alright. But they had no money to easily fix them in case of breakdowns along the way. The journey was smooth and efficient without such breakdowns. All they had was money for fuel and money collected from these passengers forming part of their business profits. In case of breakdowns, the journey took unnecessarily too long. One labour migrant, Masuzgo (troubles), indicated that in 1994 he travelled to South Africa using these local transporters and instead of taking the usual and standard two to three days, their journey took close to three weeks. This was the first trip of a certain Mr. Mwanza from Mzimba District in Malawi. Mr. Mwanza was largely inexperienced as an independent transporter between Malawi and South Africa.

In addition to breakdowns along the way, the trip was complicated and elongated by the fact that Mr. Mwanza did not have enough money as a cushion to attend to problems that arose along the way. Since it was his first time, he faced a lot of challenges trying to buy his way and that of his passengers at the border posts. Some of the documents for his lorry were not valid and he did not have a special permit to transport people. His lorry was suitable for carrying *katundu* (goods) and not passengers. It would have been easier if he was transporting people using a mini-bus, which is a passenger vehicle. Since he had already embarked on the journey, he could not turn back, but rather had to make efforts to forge ahead and still reach his destination, South Africa. In order to do this, he relied on getting small amounts of *ngongole* (loans) from his very passengers, promising to pay them upon arrival in South Africa. Most such local transporters hardly made it far in their business because they failed to win the confidence of their passengers and the latter, through word of mouth, discredited such transporters to other potential passengers.

Masuzgo only stayed for nine months in South Africa after which he decided to return to Malawi. He argued he had thought that life was going to be easy in South Africa, the much-talked-about land of opportunities. However, upon arrival, he realized that life was not that easy. He struggled to secure a job and was not even satisfied with the type of job he had secured: working as a watchman for a certain security organization. He compared this with his life back home and came to the painful conclusion that life back home in Malawi was relatively better off. It was upon this realization that he decided to return home and continue with his life of doing small-scale businesses at societal level. During his return trip, Masuzgo used the same transporter, Mr. Mwanza. Masuzgo recounted that during this return trip they faced even worse problems than when they were going to South Africa:

When I was returning home (to Malawi) we took three weeks. We had several breakdowns along the way. We started off in South Africa and this time we went via Botswana and Zambia. Since he had a lot of problems with the immigration and customs officials, I was appointed a team leader *de facto*. This was because I was the most literate member amongst the labour migrants: I could talk to border officials while Mr. Mwanza was trying to process our travel documents with the immigration officials. At times he could be taken away by the traffic police, for example, in Botswana and Zambia and during such occasions I was virtually in charge of the group. It was during the rainy season and we eventually reached Malawi dirty (muddy) and exhausted. We could hardly take a bath all those days and we survived on drinks and two slices of bread in a day. After we arrived at home, I swore never to go back to South Africa gain.

Masuzgo actually concluded that although South Africa is renowned as a land of opportunities, what actually happens there is not all rosy: Some people end up struggling and leading very miserable lives right there in South Africa. In his case, he maintained that he had never expected to work as a watchman in this 'land of opportunities'.

In the early 1990s transporters established booking offices in the departure districts in Malawi from where passengers bought tickets. They were then told about a departure day, usually two weeks away. At that point, having secured their seat, they went back home to make final preparations for the impending journey. In some cases, especially when many people were to start off from an area, they could be promised to be picked at a central point, for instance, a trading centre in their home area. In Mzimba District, such collection points would be such places as Eswazini in Traditional Authority (T.A.) Kampingo Sibande or Manyamula, Engalaweni, Chiseng'ezi or the popular Zubayumo Makamo area in T.A. M'mbelwa. This arrangement was an additional attraction of local transport and also why migrants preferred it over the more comfortable buses and coaches.

Booking offices were popular together with telephone bureaux since in those days cell phones were not yet popular. This was partly because these cell phones were still very expensive and also because cell phone network coverage was still limited. Most places in the rural areas were not covered by network. Hence people still relied on telephone services. Most people including returning labour migrants made huge investments in these telephone bureaux. They used these bureaux to communicate with the transport operators and arrange their journeys to South Africa. After fixing departures dates, passengers relied on these telephone bureaux to find out in case there were any changes to the departure programme.

After embarking on this long journey to South Africa, whatever happened along the way tended to differ from previous journeys and was actually unique in itself. Because of the unpredictability of such journeys, it was rather difficult for labour migrants to adequately prepare for the trips. The transport operators were not providing food and accommodation along the way, hence the shorter the trip, the better. On average, such journeys to South Africa used to take two or three days. But this hardly was the case since there were usually hurdles along the way. Hence if, for one reason or another, the trip took longer than the anticipated three days all the pocket money would be used up and thereafter passengers suffered a great deal. They usually relied on giving each other in the group some small *ngongole* and promising to pay back upon arrival in South Africa. They also used to share the little foodstuffs they carried along and whatever they could manage to buy along the way, in Mozambique and in Zimbabwe, before finally entering South Africa. Since most were traveling for the first time, it was their relatives (brothers, cousins and uncles) who were settling the *ngongole* on their behalf in South Africa.

Apart from the problem of food provisions along the way, there are nasty stories associated with accommodation challenges along the way. Due to unforeseen breakdowns, migrants traveling to South Africa would sometimes be forced to spend a week at a certain place. During such crises, there are stories of women falling victim at the hands of unscrupulous transporters. The latter would promise to provide for the food and accommodation needs of these stranded female passengers usually in exchange for sex. In dire need of subsistence, at times these passengers would have no option but to oblige. At times the transporter would deliberately book a single room with a single bed to be shared between the transporter himself and one of the female passengers. The end result would be the transporter achieving his desire and plan of sleeping with the female passenger.

Some of these female passengers would be married women traveling to South Africa to visit their husbands working there. In some cases it would be male and female passengers sleeping with each other during these periods of prolonged breakdowns in exchange for food, accommodation and other types of favours.

The other serious problem occurred just upon arrival in South Africa. When starting off from Malawi local transporters promised male and female migrants that they would be handed over to their relatives right at the residential places of their relatives (door step delivery). However, upon arrival, these transporters would keep these passengers for a couple of days at their own homes, arguing they were failing to link up with the migrants' (passengers') relatives in South Africa. During these days the transporters would be doing them a favour by offering them food and accommodation, but those transporters with ill motives usually took advantage of this 'crisis' and sleep with one or some of the female migrants. This usually happens when female migrants are going to South Africa for the very first time. These migrants would really be in a fix since they do not yet know anyone and any place in South Africa.

Some of these female migrants would be forced to sleep with these transporters without their consent but would have nowhere to report to in a totally new and strange place. In addition, these transporters would instil fear in them, arguing they would be arrested and deported back to Malawi if they dared report the matter to the police; that the latter are already on the look-out for illegal migrants. Yet this would not be true since just upon arrival, the first-time immigrants into South Africa are still legal migrants as they are given a 30-day visa upon entry at Beitbridge Border Post. As for married women, they would not dare report these rape cases to their husbands for fear of losing their bona fide marriages. This is one instance through which couples end up infecting their partners with HIV that causes AIDS.

In extreme and bizarre cases, there are stories bordering on human trafficking whereby female migrants transported by these local transporters are actually auctioned in such high residential areas like Diepsloot, Honeydew and Alexandra in South Africa. These female migrants are promised jobs in Malawi and also to be handed over to their relatives upon arrival. But to their shock and dismay, they are offered for auction sale to Malawian migrants residing in South Africa. If there are two bidders, the highest bidder, say with R3000, ends up taking the female migrant away, just like what typically happens in a normal auction sale. In some cases, this happens after the transporters themselves have already slept with these women. There are stories that in the above residential areas in South Africa there are designated places where these local truck and bus operators park on particular known days in a week. Hence these Malawian migrants usually flock to such places to 'buy' female migrants, take them away in the name of assisting them with food and accommodation. But, in actual fact, they take them away as their suitors or sex partners.

There are also better scenarios where such stranded male and female migrants are handed over to various welfare societies and Malawian churches in South Africa. The leadership of these welfare societies make efforts to link these migrants to their relatives and this is usually easy because migrants have vibrant welfare societies and most migrants are members of these societies. Although there are many such societies, leaders of these societies have strong links and are, therefore, able to establish the respective migrants' relatives in South Africa.

As for churches, the migrants who have been handed over to them are introduced to church members during the Sunday prayer service during which the Reverend makes an effort to announce their names, and where they are coming from in Malawi, and the names of their relatives in South Africa. After this kind gesture, relatives or mere well-wishers come forward to offer these stranded migrants a home and food. They also promise to assist them to look for some temporary jobs to keep them busy, before they, themselves, can ably secure a better-paying job once they get established. In general, cases of abuse of female migrants by these well-wishers are minimal, especially when these migrants have been handed over to the church. The latter also takes a keen interest on the welfare of these stranded migrants afterwards. In addition, most of these well-wishers are devout members of these churches.

There are also a number of stories regarding problems encountered by migrants on the way to South Africa. Such stories are associated with buses operated by individuals and not established bus companies. Unlike the latter, these individually-owned buses encounter a lot of problems along the way. Most of them are not roadworthy since some vehicle documents are expired or outdated. Hence they are frequently impounded by the traffic police. It so happens that a bus may be impounded say five times by different traffic policemen between Malawi and South Africa. During each scenario the driver has to buy his way through palm-oiling, that is, bribing the police officers. This becomes a trend or practice until they reach the destination. In some cases they stay one full day or two at a place before they are released. This ultimately contributes to delays along the way. Consequently, instead of spending a few days they spend many days along the way. Despite this, the bus owner does not alleviate the passengers' suffering by providing them with basics like food and accommodation. All this responsibility is shouldered by the passengers, themselves.

Such stories associated with various local bus operators are collectively referred to here as the 'Chinjoka bus stories'. Chinjoka bus service is one popular local bus operated by Malawians. This bus is very popular in northern Malawi and, especially, in Mimba District, a popular labour migration district in the country. The bus operates from Mzuzu City (northern Malawi) to Johannesburg. In Mzuzu, it transports mainly the Tonga from Nkhata-Bay District, a lakeshore, equally-popular labour migration area in northern Malawi. The Tonga have a long history of emigrating to South Africa for wage employment. During the old migration period (1880-1980s), the Tonga were renowned for emigrating to South Africa largely under *selufu*.

From Mzuzu City, the bus' next major stop is Mzimba District before proceeding all the way to South Africa through Lilongwe, Malawi's Capital City. In Mzimba the bus takes a large number of Ngoni migrants from the district. Despite numerous problems along the way, the bus has for many years been popular because of low transport fares. The other advantage is that the bus operators take on board all travellers whether they have valid travel documents or not. In case they have invalid papers, it is the duty of the bus operators to see to it that they negotiate with immigration authorities until all the passengers reach South Africa.

In some cases the passengers are told to add a little amount of money on top of the transport fare and this is the money used to buy the passengers' way to South Africa. In such cases, the attraction of such local buses as Chinjoka is not in the low transport fare, but the guarantee that the passengers on board will reach their ultimate destination, South Africa. The other comparative advantage with other more established bus services is that these local buses, just like the local lorry transport services, provide a door-to-door delivery service, that is, the passengers are taken all the way to either their relatives' residential places or to a central location close to these areas.

The problem with such local buses is that they tend to avoid main routes or highways and opt for some short-cuts or earth roads in trying to avoid problems with the traffic police. The saying 'a short-cut is always a long cut' fully applies to these local buses. They consequently end up taking longer, that is, more days than anticipated. In addition, some of these roads are not in good condition, hence they get stuck in the mud days on end, especially during the rainy season. There are also stories of passengers aboard these local buses and lorries drowning in big rivers like Limpopo between Zimbabwe and South Africa as they try to avoid entering South Africa at the main entry point, Beitbridge Border Post. Apart from merely drowning, rivers like Limpopo are full of crocodiles and there have been cases of passengers being killed by crocodiles. This usually happens because the bus and lorry transport operators off-load passengers close to police road blocks and encourage them to cross on foot and arrange to pick them up after these road barriers. It is during this short stint that these passengers meet their fate (i.e. drowning and being killed by dangerous crocodiles while crossing rivers).

During trips through these bushes there have also been incidents of passengers being intercepted by armed robbers and thieves who lie in waiting and eventually ambush the passengers using these trails in the thick bushes. This is very common when crossing Mozambique, Zimbabwe and entering South Africa in areas close to Beitbridge Border Post. These armed robbers attack and snatch all their possessions like electronic gadgets including cell phones and cameras. Some of these robbers also rape female migrants as passengers scatter in different directions following such attacks. In this connection, there have also been cases whereby passengers have ended up suspecting the owners of these buses, in view of how planned these attacks appear to be carried out. There are allegations that some of these attacks might be part of a syndicate involving these robbers and bus operators with the aim of stealing from the unsuspecting passengers.

In a recent and related development, it was reported in July 2017 in the print and electronic media about the Ingwenya Bus Scandal. Ingwenya Bus Service is a little-known bus service operated by Zimbabweans between Malawi and South Africa. In July 2017 this bus was involved in dubious and shady deals that bordered on human trafficking, smuggling and kidnapping. The passengers were requested to pay additional money on top of the money for buying passenger tickets. This additional money was meant to buy passengers' way *en route* to South Africa. However, along the way, in Zimbabwe to be precise, the bus was diverted into the bushes, where all passengers were commanded to communicate with their relations in South Africa, who were supposed to bail them out by depositing prescribed amounts of money into specified bank accounts. All those whose relatives deposited the money were freed, while the rest were harassed in different ways including actual beating. This was typical kidnapping like what happens in the action movies.

One of the victims on board this bus, but who got released after his relatives bailed him out, circulated a video clip on electronic media and this was partly what led to the incident becoming a hot and trending scandal on social media. This revelation led to the arrest of a number of employees working for this bus in *Wenela* Bus premises in Malawi's major commercial district of Blantyre. What follows here is a lengthy excerpt of the video clip that the Good Samaritan in question posed on social media, calling for the immediate intervention and action by the relatives of the passengers aboard the bus in question.

I am one of the people who boarded a bus called Ingwenya on 12 July 2017. The office for this bus company is close to Petroda Filling Station at Clock Tower in Blantyre. At this place there is a sign that reads "African Coaches". The owner of this office is known by the name John (not real name). I went to their office and bought a ticket to South Africa at K33,000.00. But they also requested that we pay an additional R1,000 (K50,000) which they would use to assist us with anything we would need along the way. I also paid this money. It seems that many other passengers were made to pay this additional amount. But what was surprising is that after we boarded the bus, John, the owner, was nowhere to be seen. "Where is John?" People asked to no avail. So we started off for South Africa, but there was no one to help us in case of problems along the way. This was despite the additional R1,000 we had paid.

We learnt that the bus company is from Zimbabwe and, in fact, the owner was right inside the bus: a fat, short man. He was just quiet; never said anything while we, the passengers, were facing different kinds of problems. As for me, I was a bit lucky since I had some spare money in my pocket and I was using this money to deal with problems, but, for the other passengers, they were suffering a lot because they did not have additional money.

The other problem was that this bus used to break down a lot. We departed from Blantyre, Malawi, on Wednesday, but we stayed too long in Zimbabwe. By Saturday, we were still in Zimbabwe, quite a long way from South Africa. But on Saturday night the bus stopped at a certain place and next to this place was parked a Quantum Toyota mini-bus with tinted glasses. They took us out of the bus and into this mini-bus. However, the people we found in this mini-bus were clearly "*anthu oti amwa mankhwala ozunguza bongo*" (people under the influence of intoxicating drugs). They were shouting and had put on long jackets and there were indications that they had guns. So we never posed any resistance. In their view, they wanted to assist us to cross Beitbridge Border Post using the mini-bus.

But we were surprised that they took us to a certain thick forest, where there was no water and food. There we found Zimbabwean soldiers who were heavily armed. But when all this was happening, we kept our cool. Eventually, they requested us, passengers, to surrender to them cell phone numbers of our relatives in South Africa. After we gave them these numbers, they started calling our relatives, telling them that they will give them bank account numbers so that they deposit money in order to bail us out. They told them that we had been kidnapped.

For those whose relatives were not picking up the phone calls, they were being beaten severely. But for those of us whose relatives picked up the phone calls and immediately deposited the money requested, we were spared the wrath. In my case, my relatives deposited the money and it reflected on their phone that the money had, indeed, been deposited. In the evening of the same day, they took all of us into another vehicle and they took us to Johannesburg. Here they locked us up in a certain house. They continued to torture those whose relatives had not yet deposited the money. It was very sad to see people being beaten mercilessly. But for those whose relatives had deposited the money, they told them that they were free to leave. The other sad thing is that women were being harassed: touching their buttocks, etc.

What I want is that those who get this message should quickly report this to any nearest police station in Malawi. You may have relatives who took this Ingwenya Bus on that day and may not have reached their destination and you may be wondering as to why. We left some passengers right in the forest, whereas others in the house in Johannesburg, actually being beaten mercilessly. You can't tell, some may even have been killed. So it's better to report to police in Malawi. Upon inquiry, I learnt that this bus was banned in Zimbabwe because of its human trafficking activities. In fact, people stopped using this bus. That is why they relocated to Malawi. So we also need to fight hard so that its operations are also banned in Malawi. In addition, their offices in *Wenela*, Blantyre, have to be investigated. Malawians should be encouraged to use Intercape and Munorurama buses; the rest of the buses indulge in human trafficking. Please help in spreading this message.

In addition to loss of property as a result of such organized attacks by robbers, there are numerous cases of passengers' goods getting lost along the way. There are frequent incidents of petty thefts by thieves at border posts. These thieves steal either wallets from the passengers' pockets or steal small bags from inside the bus at border posts by disguising themselves as passengers on board these buses. Since border posts are usually jam-packed with passengers going to different destinations, especially during the festive seasons like the Christmas period, the passengers only realize afterwards that they are missing wallets or money. Unfortunately, reporting to police authorities does not yield any results since they can hardly identify the culprits due to overcrowding.

The other problem with local buses and lorries has to do with delays before starting off either in South Africa for Malawi or in Malawi for South Africa. The transport operators inform passengers about the departure day, but when that day comes they start telling stories: that they are not ready to start off and keep on postponing the departure day. They inform passengers that the bus is full when in fact it is half empty. Hence this dilly-dallying is meant to ensure that the bus is full. This takes a couple of extra days and even a week at most. This makes life of migrants difficult as they are forced to camp at the departure point for all that period. This means fending for themselves in terms of food and accommodation for this entire waiting period. Although these local buses and lorries are cheaper than the more established coaches like Intercape and Munorurama, they prove to be more expensive because they do not operate in line with fixed schedules. For instance, a one-way trip on the established coaches would cost R1,400 while the local buses would charge R1,000. But in practice the passenger on the local buses would spend more, say R1,600, before reaching Malawi or South Africa. All this is a result of unforeseen delays.

The same problem applies to buses and lorries starting off from Malawi to South Africa. Their departure depends on whether they are full or not. If all the seats are sold in a short period of time, then they depart quickly, otherwise the same waiting period applies. The only difference and solace, though, is that when departing from Malawi passengers wait from their homes and hence they incur less additional costs. However, a few days before the actual departure, they still have to move closer to the departure points, hence in the process incurring some costs, though relatively minimal. As for the local lorry transporters, they have small pick-up trucks which move around the villages collecting migrants on the trip and bringing them to the departure points. The problem is that they are not sincere to tell their passengers the actual travel programme.

Unlike established coach companies which have a fleet of coaches, local buses struggle during breakdowns. As for established buses, they easily field another replacement bus in case of breakdowns or accidents. But for the local buses, hell breaks loose in case of such eventualities. They strive to fix the problem before the journey either to Malawi or to South Africa can continue. Depending on the severity of the breakdown, this may take from a few days to a week before continuing with the journey. Such companies like Chipozani Coaches only have two buses operating between Malawi and South Africa. Both buses operate simultaneously, though on different days, hence there is a fix during breakdowns. Tilitose, one of the migrants who once travelled using Chipozani Coaches, indicated that they once spent four days in Mozambique before the breakdown could be fixed:

When I was traveling from Malawi to South Africa one day we had a breakdown in Mozambique. It took them three days to fix the problem and we only continued with the journey on the fourth day. We really suffered: We had problems with a place where to sleep and take a bath. In terms of food, the owners of the bus were providing us with one meal per day and for the rest of the day we minded our own business. What they usually do is that during such incidents, they call for their mechanics who are based in South Africa and in Malawi. So it depends on the accident or breakdown point: If the breakdown has occurred close to Malawi, say in Mozambique, mechanics come from Malawi. If the breakdown has occurred in Zimbabwe, mechanics usually come from Johannesburg. The problem is that whatever the case, it takes a while for these mechanics to arrive at the breakdown spot.

Most buses and lorries start off from Johannesburg's Park Station when departing for Malawi. However, others, especially the local buses start off from the residential areas which have a huge Malawian migrant population. These include Diepsloot and Honeydew. From there they head to Beitbridge Border where passengers cross to Zimbabwe Border. Thereafter, they cross Zimbabwe and exit it at Nyamapanda Border. At this point, they enter Mozambique and travel across it and eventually enter Malawi either through Dedza or Mwanza borders. Hence in short, there are six borders in total between Malawi and South Africa. Consequently, one major problem that migrants face are delays at these borders since passengers have to clear their travel documents, for instance, passports and *katundu* (goods') receipts with the immigration and custom officers, respectively. This process of clearing documents usually takes long as there are many buses and pick-up trucks at these borders at any time of the day.

On particular days like Saturdays and Wednesdays, at times there are seven buses, all heading towards one direction: either to South Africa or Malawi. In addition, there are heavy goods trucks also passing through the same borders and whose drivers are equally looking for means of fast clearance. This scenario automatically brings into the picture elements or incidents of corruption. It starts with the bus stewards. Since the journey between Malawi and South Africa on average takes two days, the bus drivers and stewards make efforts to ensure this travel time is not elongated. Hence drivers' role is to cruise very fast and minimizing the number and length of stoppages. They, therefore, stick to designated stop over points apart from stopping at border points for the usual clearance procedure.

As for the stewards or hosts, their role is to ensure that all the passengers have the required and valid documentation. This minimizes time for unnecessary delays at these borders. Hence for those passengers who have problems with their documentation, the hosts collect their passports and process the clearances on behalf of these passengers. Such documents require bribing officials, hence the passengers are required to part with some money, for example, R50 each towards this cause. Such documents are reason for delays since the hosts have to look for officials with whom they are friends to do the clearance. This is usually done secretly and there is sometimes need to wait until all the passengers with valid documents have been cleared. With a number of passengers having expired documents, and on a day with as many buses as seven heading in one direction, either to Malawi or South Africa, clearance at one border post takes an average of four hours instead of the usual average of one hour. Cumulatively, this has an overall impact on the total travel time. Instead of taking the usual one-and-half days, such delays may result in a journey lasting two or three days. Details on the delays at the border posts come under chapter three on institutionalized corruption.

In 2015 and 2016 infighting between the Mozambican government and the opposition side, Renamo, resumed. Because of the disagreements between the two sides following the general elections, Renamo decided to go into physical fighting with the government side. Reports indicate the disagreement followed dispute over regions each side was to control in Mozambique. Renamo was seemingly an aggressor in this dispute since it quickly resorted to fighting before the negotiations were thoroughly concluded. This action by Renamo in trying to control the northern Mozambican region had a deleterious impact on the operations of public transport transiting through Mozambique between Malawi and South Africa. Within a few weeks and months there were reports of opposition Renamo soldiers attacking public transport like buses and pick-up trucks. The main aim was to make their action felt by the government. Such guerrilla attacks on innocent passengers led to some migrants losing their lives or being maimed in the process.

There were some reports of Renamo and Mozambican government soldiers attacking such public transport and killing everybody on board. Even personal cars fell victim of such attacks. The latter were followed by wanton looting of all the passengers' possessions. At the peak of such attacks, some transporters were forced to temporarily cancel their business schedules in order to avoid such eventualities. The social media also assisted in instilling fear in the potential travellers who, consequently, postponed their trips. Hence these transporters were forced to cancel trips because of low turn up of passengers willing to use road transport between Malawi and South Africa. In addition, some transport operators were forced by such circumstances to change their routes: going through Botswana and Zambia in trying to avoid the then dangerous Mozambique territory. Some travellers were affected in the sense that they were compelled to resort to air transport despite the known fact that flights are very expensive. All this was the inconvenience and suffering to which the war in Mozambique subjected innocent migrants and traders traveling between Malawi and South Africa.

Traders' Experiences between Malawi and South Africa

Unlike labour migrants who have been traveling to South Africa for wage employment since the 1880s, traders, doing business in various items, started going to South Africa during the new or contemporary period. Hence their experiences or challenges during their journeys to and from South Africa are largely traced back to the early 1990s. However, in addition to South Africa Malawian traders have been going to Tanzania and Zimbabwe to buy various merchandise for resale in Malawi. Of these three countries, it is the trade with Tanzania that is more established. As for the trade between Malawi and Zimbabwe, it was vibrant for the first ten years following the introduction of multi-party politics in Malawi in 1994. However, this trade collapsed following the faltering of Zimbabwe's economy as a result of the continued mal-administration under the tutelage of President Robert Mugabe.

The once-mighty and vibrant Zimbabwe's economy is a thing of the past. Going through Zimbabwe's capital, Harare, one really comes face to face with wanton destruction and dilapidation of one of the then most beautiful cities in Africa. There is filth everywhere and the tarred roads are but in shambles. In my view, the only business still thriving in major cities in Zimbabwe are filling stations, garages and eating places since travellers in transit still need such services. No wonder most traders from Malawi simply take Zimbabwe as a transit corridor and conduit to South Africa.

Since 2005 trade in small merchandise between Malawi and Zimbabwe virtually collapsed. This is unbelievable since a decade prior to 2005 Zimbabwe was a source of almost every small trade commodity that was rare in Malawi. At some point Malawian traders went to Zimbabwe to procure such items as fresh milk, tomatoes, margarine and eggs. One wonders why such items as eggs should be bought from as far as Zimbabwe. Does it mean that Malawi was failing to rear chickens to ensure adequate supply of eggs on the market? But surprisingly, this was a hot and profitable business for Malawian small-scale traders. After 2005 some companies looked at the high demand for eggs and other items and decided to establish some locally-based companies specializing in those items on high demand. This development brought about stability and coupled with the economic woes in Zimbabwe, trade with Zimbabwe died down.

For so many years, Malawian traders have been relying on Tanzania as a viable source of trade items such as clothes, shoes and cooking oil. Much of this trade has been concentrated in Tanzanian towns close to Malawi's bordering districts of Chitipa and Karonga at the northern tip of Malawi. Such towns include Rembuka and Usale and, as a result, the resultant business in northern Malawi in items procured from such towns is popularly known after such towns, hence Rembuka or Usale business. This trade is concentrated mainly between these Tanzanian towns and northern Malawi districts, especially with Karonga, the border district, and Mzuzu, the city in northern Malawi. In addition to clothes, during lean months when local supply shrinks, Tanzania is annually the source of alternative Irish potatoes. The latter, however, are of lower quality as compared to the more nutritious and tasteful Irish potatoes locally grown in Malawi, especially in Jenda area in Mzimba District and in parts of Dedza and Ntcheu districts in central Malawi.

Although trade between Malawi and Tanzania is still thriving and vibrant, it is the trade in various items between Malawi and South Africa that has taken centre stage. This is a result of the fact that South Africa has a vibrant manufacturing industry, hence it is a source of various manufactured products not produced locally in Malawi. This business is facilitated by a reliable and established road transport network between these two countries. Malawi's manufacturing base became weak in the 1990s following the privatization of most manufacturing companies. Hence the most reliable alternative source of manufactured goods were South Africa and Zimbabwe. But after the collapse of Zimbabwe's economy in the 2000s only South Africa remained as a major source of such products.

Just like labour migrants, traders doing business between the two countries face a lot of problems *en route* to and from South Africa. Although these problems are largely the same as those of labour migrants, there are a few differences For instance, the problem of migrants overstaying in South Africa and, therefore, traveling with expired visas does not apply to traders. The latter are more mobile so much so that they come back to Malawi after buying their trade items before the expiry of their allocated 30-day visas. Put differently, they always have a clean record, that is, valid visas and passports. But this does not mean that these traders do not face problems along the way. They face a lot of problems but of a different kind and nature from those of labour migrants.

Most of these traders have problems with their trade items: having them cleared by the custom officials at various borders. In other words, while migrants have problems clearing their travel documents with immigration officials, traders have challenges clearing *katundu* (goods) with customs officials. This is because the duty that is charged upon entry into Malawi at Dedza Border or Mwanza Border is very exorbitant so that they hardly make meaningful profits. As a result, they are compelled to devise survival strategies. The latter include befriending some customs officials so that they should be getting some favours and duty waiver on some items. There are stories of traders who are fond of finding out on which days in a particular week their friends, that is, customs officers, will be on duty and making deliberate efforts to pass through Dedza or Mwanza borders on those specified days. This includes deliberately delaying their departure dates from South Africa for Malawi.

Although clearing trade items is a rigorous process since buses and trucks are usually full of these trade items and also because there are many such buses and trucks at a time, there is a lot of time wasted on these two borders as business men and women enter into lengthy negotiations with officials for a reduction in custom duty charged on their goods. At Dedza, for instance, an average custom clearing session usually takes three hours, but in practice buses take up to five hours before all the goods are cleared and duty duly paid for. This usually happens at the expense of other travellers like labour migrants whose *katundu* does not attract any kind of duty. Consequently, while labour migrants are the cause of delays at such borders as Beitbridge as they try to negotiate with immigration officers for entry into South Africa, at Mwanza and Dedza borders it is the traders who are behind these delays as they try to negotiate for reduced duty on their goods as they are entering Malawi.

Apart from making friends with custom officers, these traders also resort to offering these officers part of their items for their home use and consumption in exchange for favours. For instance, a businessman or woman may be carrying twenty-five cartons of apples and would be ready to part with one carton under this arrangement in order to 'buy' favours on custom duty charges. Others act as agents of these officers; the latter sending traders to buy items for them in addition to what they already purport to buy. When they reach the border, it is also time to hand over some of the items bought to the rightful owner: the custom officer in question. As can be deduced from this arrangement, it would be extremely difficult or virtually impossible for the custom officer 'to burn the hand that actually feeds him'.

In some instances, these traders simply resort to indulging in corrupt practices with the concerned officers. The latter pretend to be doing their job professionally in the eyes of the inquisitive and curious public, when in fact, after physically inspecting the goods, the payment voucher that is finally prepared and handed over to the business men and women is slashed, whereupon part of the remaining money is paid to the officer as a bribe. The other way is actually the trader under-declaring the value of trade items they are carrying and the duty is calculated not on the actual value, but on this under-declared value. Consequently, the traders pay less duty on large amounts of goods carried. These are some of the many ways how Malawi keeps on losing precious income from the many goods entering the country. Being land-locked, Malawi is supposed to be getting a lot of income from custom dues since a huge percentage of manufactured goods is externally procured.

These traders usually go to South Africa to buy goods in bulk for resale in Malawi. These goods are largely in the form of manufactured goods since South Africa has a huge and vibrant manufacturing sector. Such goods as electronic equipment like music systems, video and television screens, laptops, digital cameras and video recorders; and housewares such as refrigerators and cookers; and also house and office furniture like sofa sets, office desks feature prominently amongst the merchandise bought. The traders either have shop outlets in the major towns and cities like Zomba, Blantyre, Lilongwe and Mzuzu or operate using customer requests or orders. In line with the latter, they go to South Africa to buy goods on request and upon arrival in Malawi they merely distribute the items to the owners. When going to South Africa they demand part payment and request their customers to either complete payment upon delivery of goods or pay through two or three instalments, depending on the price of the item: the higher the price the more the number of instalments.

However, problems come in following loss of property through vehicle accidents and thefts. While these traders incur huge losses through such unforeseen circumstances, the owners of the property in Malawi expect delivery of requested items. In such cases, traders are forced to get *ngongole* (loans) in order to replace lost or damaged items. However, there are customers who are understanding and realize that whatever happened was beyond the traders' control. Such situations are unavoidable. In addition, some items get lost along the way in case the bus trailers and goods trucks are not able to accommodate all the goods. In this case, some goods are left behind. In case the owner goes to Malawi and leaves part of the items behind, it becomes difficult for the goods to arrive safely in the absence of the owner. However, this scenario too is usually unavoidable since each trader buys a lot of goods. In some cases, the bus and truck operators limit the goods that one passenger may load onto the bus or truck per trip. Any excess goods are transported to Malawi during the subsequent trips.

The other losses are to do with the many road accidents along the way. These accidents usually occur on the journey from Johannesburg to Malawi due to overloading of goods.

Although traffic policemen check the load carried, it is easy for drivers to manoeuvre their way past the many road blocks through bribing these traffic officers. During some fatal accidents close to trading centres and residential areas, the people along roads pounce on these vehicles and loot a lot of precious items. By the time the police and traffic officers arrive at the accident scene, it is usually too late. This tendency is usually associated with bus operators which operate heavy duty trucks specifically to transport traders' goods. The truck is usually manned by two people, a driver and his assistant, and it is usually difficult for the two to take care of more than twenty tonnes of goods, especially during accidents. During the latter, at times there arises the need to report the accident to the police. Hence this is done by one of the two people, leaving only one person to look after these goods. The situation becomes tricky if these two people (driver and assistant) have been hurt in the course of the accident.

Photograph 2: Labour migrants' and traders' *katundu* (goods) being off-loaded for checking and determination of customs duty at Dedza Border Post; entry into Malawi (photo by author).

Photograph 3: Ingwenya Bus Service embroiled in a scandal bordering on kidnapping and human trafficking as it operates between Malawi and South Africa. Date of the scandal trip from Malawi to South Africa was 12 July 2017 (source: Facebook images/ posts).

Chapter Three

Institutionalized Corruption

Corruption, variously described in northern Malawi as *vimbundi* and *katangale*, is one of the worst practices affecting the development agenda of many countries in the world. This practice is so entrenched in most African countries that it has become a demeanour (order of the day) instead of being, rightly, a misdemeanour. In most countries the corruption rot is traced at every level of the hierarchy in both public and private sectors. There seems to be no end in sight for corrupt tendencies because it is rebuked on paper only whereas in practice the mindset is 'as long as I am the beneficiary, all other concerns can wait'. How can corruption be uprooted in a country where all the three arms of the government (the executive, the judiciary and the parliament) are filthy corrupt? This is plainly and simply not possible. The judiciary and the police, including the various anti-corruption agencies, are in most cases in the forefront practising corruption underground and yet on the surface they are busy pretending to be advancing the anti-corruption agenda.

Countries like Malawi, Zambia, Zimbabwe, Kenya and South Africa feature highly on the corruption index in Africa. Of late the only country which is an exception in the region is Tanzania. After President Magufuli was elected president, he cracked down on all elements of corruption, taking to task all corrupt government officials. A good number of civil servants have since been arrested or fired from their positions. In Malawi, one of the presidents who masterminded the anti-corruption drive during the multi-party dispensation is Dr.

Bingu wa Mutharika and yet the irony of it is that one of the biggest corruption scandals in the country came to the surface during his reign. While he was busy with the anti-corruption rhetoric, his officers in the civil service were but busy amassing wealth illegally for themselves. In fact, after his demise, there were stories, right or wrong, of huge sums of money illegally found at his newly-built mansion. Although such stories are mere fabrications by his haters, there is also this old adage in Chitumbuka *'pali bii, pali munga'* which in English might be equated to the saying 'there is no smoke without fire'.

In Malawi widespread corruption in the country is traced back to the inception of multi-party politics in 1994. Although in the pre-1994 period there might equally have been elements of corruption, the situation was under control. Under the reign of Dr. Hastings Kamuzu Banda, Malawi's first president, people were afraid to indulge in malpractices, bearing in mind that anyone found against the law was harshly dealt with. But since 1994 people misunderstood freedoms and democracy. To them, these meant one being free to do whatever one liked. Eventually, this even came to mean people not being afraid of committing criminal activities. It is during this period that various terminologies associated with corruption and bribery were coined: *viphuphu, vimbundi, katangale,* among others.

Bakili Muluzi's regime between 1994 and 2004 came to be associated with all kinds of evils and rot in society. His populist politics was responsible for ushering in laziness in the minds of the populace. The latter came to believe that the government would provide all their needs through food and money handouts. While this was meant by Bakili Muluzi to woo people's support and their confidence during the general elections, it eroded the hard-working spirit that for a long time was characteristically associated with Malawians. Although he encouraged Malawians to venture into different types of small-scale businesses as part of income-generation, as a result of this laziness people came to rely on short-cuts and corruption as a sure way towards quick and ill-begotten wealth. As a result, during business transactions almost everybody expected some kind of kick-backs or favours. By 2004 when Dr. Mutharika was taking over leadership, the rot in society had reached a point of no return. No wonder some academicians have referred to the period between 1994 and 2004 as the lost decade in Malawi's democratic history.

In spite of this, it is the same decade that is associated with business men and women opening up and realizing the huge business potential between Malawi and other countries in the region. Although most traders were already plying their business with Tanzania to the north, they started exploring other business avenues and in the process began doing business first with Zimbabwe and, after a short while, with the land of unlimited opportunities, South Africa. Although business between Malawi and Zimbabwe in cheap items was vibrant, it was short-lived. This was a result of the weakening of the Zimbabwean currency and consequently Malawian business people started operating on losses. This compelled them to diversify their destination further, in the process discovering South Africa as a huge market potential.

Initially business between Malawi and South Africa was limited because of transport challenges. However, the business quickly boomed following the improvement in the mode of transport. Within a few years, South Africa and Zimbabwe bus companies introduced bus services all the way from South Africa to Malawi's capital city, Lilongwe. Within a short period of time, these bus services were extended to Blantyre in southern Malawi and to Mzuzu in northern Malawi. These established bus services were soon followed by local transport operators who joined the transport scene between land-locked Malawi and South Africa via Mozambique and Zimbabwe. It is this improved road transport network that facilitated easy movement not only of labour migrants, but also both male and female traders between Malawi and South Africa.

As a result of the numerous challenges that labour migrants and traders face *en route* between Malawi and South Africa, they are compelled to devise survival mechanisms. One of the latter is to resort to corruption and bribery with immigration, customs and police officers along the way. This trend has become so entrenched nowadays that corruption and bribery are the order of the day at the border posts and on the various road blocks between Malawi and South Africa. It is for this reason that I call this trend institutionalized corruption. For instance, some public transport operators indulge in such malpractices openly in public without any remorse. They even boast that corruption is one sure way as to why most policemen and women supplement their meagre salaries. The latter for such professions as the immigration and police officers is a problem that cuts across countries and regions in the world, especially in most African countries. With huge responsibility within their households, indulging in corrupt practices is the only practical and viable way out of their 'quagmire' and predicament.

Consequently, bribery and corruption are commonplace not only in Malawi and South Africa as the source and destination of migrants, respectively, but also in transit countries of Mozambique, Zimbabwe, Zambia and Botswana. It is fascinating and perturbing to note that South Africa is the one that is supposed to be scrutinizing migrants' travel documents like passports for cases of expired visas at

Beitbridge Border Post. But in practice, border officers in countries like Mozambique and Zimbabwe are equally on the forefront checking migrants' documents for expired visas - proof of overstaying in South Africa. The question here is 'of what concern is the issue of an expired visa during one's stay in South Africa to an immigration officer in Mozambique and Zimbabwe?' This is enough proof that such officers in these countries have actually taken this development as one sure way through which they make cheap money. In fact, it is a tactic they have devised to extort money from the many migrants traveling through their roads on a regular basis.

Corruption has become institutionalized from Malawi all the way to the migrants' destination, South Africa. At every point along the way one visibly sees uniformed officers indulging in corrupt practices and in broad day light at that. The first time I travelled by bus from Lilongwe, Malawi, to Johannesburg, South Africa, was in February 2005. This was the first time I personally came face to face with corruption between travellers and various government officers. The bus from Lilongwe then was full of both labour migrants and traders going to South Africa for their respective reasons: The labour migrants for wage employment and the traders for business purposes.

Since 2015 I have been going to South Africa neither as a labour migrant nor a trader, but for educational purposes. During the numerous road trips that I have been making, partly as part of my research on labour migrants from northern Malawi working in South Africa, I have come across a cross-section of labour migrants and traders either going to South Africa or to Malawi. In most cases they use coaches like Intercape, Munorurama, Chipozani and Business Times. Apart from these established coaches, there are other less-established and local coaches. The latter are cheaper but less reliable, for instance, they take many days to reach their respective destinations. In addition to using these coaches, these traders and migrants also travel using local pick-up trucks operated by Malawian local transporters. Some of these transporters were former labour migrants who invested in transport business part of their savings from years of working in South Africa. In this case, a good number of these local transport operators hail from the labour migration areas in Mzimba and Nkhata-Bay in northern Malawi. However, of these two labour migration districts, the majority of labour migrants originate from the western part of Mzimba District.

Corruption between Labour Migrants and Border Officials

Most of the labour migrants that I have usually come across are from central and northern Malawi and these board buses and lorries that go through Dedza Border in central Malawi. Most of the migrants and traders from northern Malawi are either Tonga from Nkhata-Bay District or Ngoni from Mzimba District. The migrants from central Malawi are Chewa from Lilongwe, Kasungu, and Dedza districts. As for migrants and traders from various districts in southern Malawi, they go through Mwanza Border. Most of these are Yao-speakers from districts like Mangochi, Machinga and Balaka.

It is interesting to note that the majority of labour migrants from northern Malawi prefer working in the informal sector and usually work as gardeners, cooks and cleaners within the employers' compounds. This is because of the long history of labour migration from northern Malawi to South Africa. Although in the pre-1990 period most migrants worked in the mines, a small section of these migrant workers went to South Africa under *selufu* and ended up working as domestic workers. After the decline in mine migration at the end of the 1980s, they continued working in the informal sector. As for the Chewa and the Yawo from the central region and southern region, respectively, they prefer working as shop assistants in Johannesburg and other surrounding areas. This is largely because of their background as traders. Most of them actually confessed that they have never dreamt of working as a gardener and a cook in someone's home.

Since the labour migrants' aim is to work and accumulate savings for investment back in Malawi, they usually stay longer in South Africa. Some of them stay for two or more years. There are some migrants who end up becoming *matchona* (the overstayers) in the quest of maximizing on savings. Some of them overstay as a result of merely being irresponsible, that is, neglecting their family responsibilities left behind. When they are planning to go to South Africa, they have brilliant plans. But upon arrival and after securing a good job, it is as if they are dreaming: They cannot believe that their many years of joblessness in Malawi is over. As a result, some indulge in strange behaviours: they start drinking beer excessively and womanizing. In the process all their migration goals are thrown to the dogs.

After staying for a few months in South Africa, the labour migrants have expired visas since they are usually given 30-day visas upon entry. Hence whenever they want to go back to Malawi for a brief holiday, which usually lasts one month, they have problems going through the various borders, especially Beitbridge Border Post. Consequently, they have one option and that is resorting to bribing immigration officers. Without this, their passports are stamped with overstay stamps and they cannot use the same passports when returning to South Africa. With such a record which is even recorded in the computers which are online, they are denied entry into South Africa at Beitbridge. Of late, those migrants with overstay visas are barred from entering South Africa for a period of five years. Since these migrants' occupation is working in South Africa, it becomes a matter of life and death. They are ready to do anything to ensure continued access to informal sector jobs in South Africa.

Migrants with overstay visas usually pay as much as R1,000 or more in order to make sure such an overstay record is cancelled. Personal interactions with these migrants revealed that they pay such huge sums of money for such a cancellation because the deal involves a number of immigration officers. Cancelling such a record in one passport may involve two or more officers who, once successful, end up sharing the bribe. During certain periods, for example, on 'lean' days with a few buses, these labour migrants only part with R500 for such a process. In most cases, labour migrants are ready to rectify their passport records on their way to Malawi, although such overstay records come into play when these labour migrants are returning to South Africa. Hence these officers are not as strict when migrants are returning home. In sharp contrast, they become very strict when labour migrants want to enter South Africa with such overstay visas. It was also noted that the amount of a bribe tends to be huge when migrants are leaving South Africa since immigration officials are fully aware that these migrants have got money after months and years of working and saving in South Africa. Hence in such cases trying to offer, say, R500 for such a service is usually turned down.

However, when going home labour migrants are not desperate and are ready to hold onto the little money that they have accumulated for use and investment back home. Most migrants have even retorted, thus: 'why should I pay a lot of money, say R1,500 when I am returning home. I know I overstayed but that is not enough reason why these immigration officials should exploit me in broad day light. If they want to cancel my passport, let them go ahead. I don't care; moreover I am going back home!" Such sentiments are common at Beitbridge in the buses from Johannesburg heading to Malawi. Some migrants have even challenged the immigration officials demanding huge sums of money for overstay visas, saying "I don't have that kind of money; if anything just go ahead and cancel my passport!" Consequently, even border officials are aware of this and are ready to soften up their condition, that is, to reduce the amount charged.

But when coming from Malawi and trying to enter South Africa, these migrants become desperate and are ready to do anything within their means to ensure that they are not turned back. Having come all the way from Malawi through Mozambique and Zimbabwe, being denied entry is the last thing these migrants expect to happen. Whatever money they have is dedicated to making sure they enter South Africa. Immigration and Home Affairs officials are fully aware of the migrants' and traders' state of desperation and hence they capitalize on the same. Consequently, they deliberately dilly dally when offered less money, for instance, in the range of R200 to R500, arguing the deal can hardly be fulfilled as it involves a number of officers. At this point and still in need of entry into South Africa, migrants resort to looking for *ngongole* from their friends, relatives or mere fellow passengers, promising to pay back the money upon arrival in South Africa.

In most cases fellow passengers are willing to assist a fellow passenger to ensure they all enter South Africa. In some cases

I have witnessed the extent of institutionalization of this corruption at these borders. When approaching a border post hosts or stewards actually make a formal announcement in the bus about the anticipated complications at the next border. They actually alert first time travellers about the established bribes at particular borders. On average, for instance, those with overstay stamps in their passports are expected to pay R50 at every border after entering Mozambique at Dedza Border. Since there are about four borders before Beitbridge, one is expected to part with R200 in total. However, at Beitbridge Border, the main gateway into South Africa, this bribe automatically jumps to R500 or even more. Some migrants were seen to be parting with R1,000 or R1,500 at Beitbridge.

This corrupt practice is so entrenched that at these other borders one is merely expected to slot the R50 note into his or her passport. Upon opening the passport, the immigration officer automatically knows the passport has got some kind of a problem bordering on overstaying in South Africa. You can hardly notice how they remove the note in a flash, stamp the passport and return it to the owner. All this happens within very few seconds. In case the money slotted into the passport is small, for example, a R20 note, the officer immediately puts the passport aside without stamping it and in a whisper tells the owner to "be more organized", that is, to add some more money otherwise the passport will not be stamped. Thereafter, the officer immediately switches his or her attention to the next passenger on the queue, clearly ignoring the earlier passenger. In this case, there is no space for further negotiations unless if this passenger whose passport has not been stamped waits until the very end of the clearance exercise when everyone has been attended to.

In the event that there are so many buses, such a passenger is afraid that he or she may be left behind by the bus he or she is traveling in. In trying to avoid this scenario, he or she immediately adds some more money, upon which the passport is stamped. If he or she does not have more money to add, the passenger withdraws from the queue, goes to ask fellow passengers for assistance in form of a loan or mere donation, and comes back straight to the front of the queue to have his or her passport stamped. If they are not as successful in looking for additional money, towards the end of the clearance exercise some officers simply get the small amounts of money and assist the passengers, accordingly. However, this depends on the inclination and disposition of the officer on duty. Some officers on these borders are so hard-hearted that migrants actually reach the point of cursing them: "May these corrupt officers never profit from this stolen money!" They maintain.

After announcing the kind of bribe required for a particular offence, in some coaches the hosts actually collect all the passports with money inside each passport for processing on behalf of the passengers. On paper, this is done to ensure the passengers do not spend a lot of money for a bribe, and also to cut down on time to be spent clearing these passports. In fact, these hosts actually claim that they are doing the passport owners a favour since they are friends with most immigration officers as they frequently travel between Malawi and South Africa. In this connection, Tiwonge, a host in one of the coaches had this to say on the matter:

Tipulikizgane mose. Ise ntchito yithu njakovwira imwe ma customer ghithu pa masuzgo agho mukusangana nagho muma border yayi. Muno passenger waliyose wakwenera kuti wabe na valid passport. Kweni tikuchita ivi pa umunthu withu waka kweniso kuti tileke kuchedwa pa border. Ma border nganandi kweniso ma bus nganandi. Otherwise tichedwenge chomene penepapo ise bus yithu yikwendera nyengo. Muno mu bus muli banthu bakwendera vifukwa vakupambanapambana, sono ntchiwemi yayi kuti tichedweskanenge. Banyake muno bakuchimbirira chomene sono ntchiwemi yayi kuti bachedwe chifukwa cha banthu bachoko waka. Lekani ise tikujichachizga kuti tovwirepo.

(Attention ladies and gentlemen. As hosts, our job is to look after the welfare of you, our customers, but it is not our responsibility to come to your rescue by offering any form of assistance at the borders. However, as human beings we are simply compelled to assist you to ensure that we do not take too long at a border. Each one of you is already expected to have a valid passport. There are so many buses at a border at a time and bearing in mind that there are a number of border posts, we may end up taking long. Moreover, our coach has scheduled traveling time and we need to stick to it. In addition, passengers here have their own and respective personal programmes, hence it is not fair for a few passengers to delay everyone. That is why we are forced to come in.)

At that point he asked all the passengers if they were in agreement with his wish to assist those passengers with various problems. Obviously, passengers agreed since they were afraid they would delay unnecessarily at these borders. With such a nod from everyone, Tiwonge thus approached all passengers with problems, attending to each passenger one by one and collecting a passport and a R50 note. He then informed all the concerned passengers to remain in the bus upon reaching the border. The rest of the passengers were told to proceed to have their passports stamped. It was him who had those passports stamped and afterwards he distributed them back to the owners. Through this arrangement, indeed, we spent very few minutes before continuing with the journey to South Africa.

This continued to happen at each of the four borders before reaching Beitbridge Border Post.

As we approached Beitbridge, he made a fresh announcement, saying at Beitbridge the R50 note is not enough and that they needed to ensure they spare at least R500 for such passport clearance. He further gave the concerned passengers the liberty to go ahead and process their passports on their own, if they so wished. However, he cautioned them that they needed to tread carefully since they risk being locked up as corruption is illegal. With this element of threat, most passengers were compelled to still allow the host to finish off the task at this remaining and difficult border. However, a few opted to do the passport clearance themselves. What actually happened thereafter was a matter of luck: some of those who decided to clear their passports on their own spent only R200 while others, who were not lucky, spent as much as R1,000. But for those who surrendered their passports to Tiwonge, the host, they only spent the requested R500. It was a game of chance; pure chance element.

However, after chatting with different passengers, especially those who usually overstay in South Africa, I so discovered that some of these hosts were actually in business. Apart from looking at the welfare of the passengers aboard the coaches, they were involved in a secret syndicate involving the immigration officers at the borders. It was revealed that out of every amount they request passengers to slot into their passengers, they get their share and surrender the rest to the officers. For example, if they collect a total of R5,000 from passengers for processing at Beitbridge, they get, say, R1,000 and hand over the remaining R4,000 to the immigration officer for processing. That is why, upon discovery, some passengers were reluctant to use these hosts as intermediaries, preferring to do the processing of their passports themselves.

Tiyenkhu, one of the passenger victims of this practice, vehemently complained about this syndicate during one of the trips:

These hosts pretend to be coming to our rescue by offering to assist us in clearing our passports, but in actual sense they are part and parcel of people who are exploiting us. What they do is they exaggerate the amount of a bribe and secretly keep part for themselves. In fact, it is part of an unwritten agreement between the bus operators, that is, hosts and drivers, on the one hand, and immigration officers, on the other hand. That is why, upon discovery and after getting a lot of such reports, a number of hosts and drivers have been fired from these bus companies.

In one of the coaches, management decided to relieve the hosts of their duties in the name of cutting down on operation costs. However, despite this development, the practice continued unabated, with the drivers taking over in full force the role that was earlier masterminded by the hosts. In fact, these drivers were so apologetic, pretending to be reluctant to assist these passengers. All this was to ensure that this was not reported to their authorities as they had been warned against this practice. A year later some familiar faces amongst these drivers started missing. Upon enquiry, it was discovered that they had been fired upon reports and complaints that they were involved in duping passengers in various ways.

However, for some buses this practice of hosts organizing bribes from passengers to immigration officers is so entrenched that they easily clear everyone's passport and immediately proceed with the journey. When this particular bus reaches a border, immigration officers are ready to shelve whatever they were doing and serve these "guests". As for the buses in which this practice is not practised, the immigration officers deliberately dilly dally, in the process frustrating the entire passengers in this bus with unnecessary delays. Although most travellers are against such corrupt practices, they are forced by circumstances to tow the corruption line to ensure speedy service at these borders. In some cases, it happens that all the passengers whether they have a problem or not, are ready to contribute a little something to be collectively handed over to the officer on duty on a particular day as part of "oil palming". Experience showed that when this happened you spent less than an hour at a border instead of the usual three hours on a very busy day.

While overstaying in South Africa ordinarily has to be the concern of immigration authorities at Beitbridge, some immigration officers in other border posts in Mozambique and Zimbabwe are taking advantage of the migrants' state of desperation to request bribes before clearing their passports. This largely happens when migrants and traders are traveling from Malawi to South Africa. These officers refuse to stamp migrants' passports with overstay stamps and yet this is supposed to be the concern of immigration authorities at Beitbridge Border Post. Most migrants have ended up wondering why this continues to be the case: "Why should we pay you money for you to stamp our passports? How does the issue of overstaying in South Africa concern you (immigration officers in Mozambique and Zimbabwe)?" However, all these questions usually fall on deaf ears, with immigration officers maintaining their ground, that they cannot stamp before the concerned passengers part with a little something. This shows how entrenched and institutionalized corruption has become in these transit countries.

In countries like Mozambique and Zimbabwe travellers with passports that have one problem or another, for instance, overstaying in South Africa, also face problems when the buses are crossing the numerous road blocks mounted along the way. At such road blocks in most cases you have policemen coming on board and requesting all the passengers to produce their passports, upon which physical checking ensues. Whoever is found with a problem is commanded to alight from the bus and taken to a make-shift office nearby. After about ten to twenty minutes, these passengers come back into the bus and upon enquiry they report that the officers snatched their passports and were requested to pay R50 in order to claim their passports. But the surprising thing is that these are mere police officers who have literally nothing to do with the issue of passports.

This makes it more complicated as the passengers cannot plan how much to spend along the way. It is developments like these which negatively impact on the passengers' financial situation. No wonder by the time they reach Beitbridge, where the issue of overstay is supposed to be handled, these passengers have no money left "to buy their way". As a result of this development, sometimes passengers fail to pay R1,000 or R1,500 demanded by immigration officers in order to secure entry into South Africa. They are lucky if they get assistance from fellow passengers or friends and relatives aboard a bus. Otherwise, some passengers have ended up being denied entry and virtually being sent back to Malawi. When this happens, one can just imagine how stranded such passengers become: being sent back at Beitbridge which is the entry post into South Africa. How will such passengers now find their way back home? Since Malawian migrants are expected to carry with them R3,000 for eventualities in South Africa, one thinks that such stranded passengers use the same to pay for transport from Beitbridge back to their respective homes in Malawi.

In case one does not have such money, the only possibility is that, having become destitute in a country away from home, one would be forced to look for *maganyu* (piece jobs) to find some quick money for basic survival, for instance, food and shelter before accumulating a little more for transport during the homeward journey. Such a situation would be similar to what used to happen in the olden days when, after failing to reach South Africa, *selufu* migrants were forced by circumstances to seek jobs either in Zimbabwe or Zambia. After working for a while and having accumulated some money, such migrants returned home. As expected, such migrants were considered as failed migrants back home since they reached home with little savings and in some extreme circumstances almost empty-handed. Most migrants make efforts to avoid such predicament as it is embarrassing to go home with nothing against a background of home people being full of expectations that returning migrants will bring home some measure of wealth.

In extreme circumstances, some migrants whose passports have expired visas end up being detained at Beitbridge. For those who are lucky, they are released a few hours later and are told to return to Malawi. For those who are not so lucky, they are taken to Lindela Repatriation Centre for onward deportation to Malawi. That is why most passengers regard Beitbridge as the most difficult border post. When migrants cross this very unpredictable post, they feel relieved and, in fact, it is time for celebration inside these buses. "Now I can earnestly say I am going to South Africa, now that my passport has been cleared at Beitbridge!" Exclaimed Masuzgo, with ululations from other passengers. Such comments are common when passengers are back aboard a bus which is starting off at Beitbridge for Johannesburg. Although this last stretch takes a whopping seven hours, most migrants easily cover this stretch since this is now time for them to sleep. They hardly sleep between Dedza Border and Beitbridge Border, a distance which takes a minimum of twenty hours to cross: During all this time, they are awake, thinking about what will happen at Beitbridge: Will they be allowed entry into South Africa? Or will they be turned back or detained and taken to Lindela? In short, most migrants are in suspense!

When migrants are coming from South Africa *en route* to Malawi, those with overstay visas have devised other survival strategies in order to ensure that they cross at Beitbridge with as little stress as possible. As indicated earlier on, such returning labour migrants are not ready to feel the pinch or be harassed by immigration officials bearing in mind that they are on a homeward journey. "These people really harass and exploit us. But it makes some sense when we are entering South Africa, not when we are going home!" Nkhwachi said loudly during one of the trips from Johannesburg to Malawi. This view is shared by many Malawian migrants with expired visas. Consequently and in order to avoid harassment, they resort to "jumping the border" by alighting from the bus before Beitbridge and walking on foot across Beitbridge Border. In this case, they are classified as pedestrians just like many migrants of Zimbabwe origin. After crossing over and while on the Zimbabwe Border side, they catch the same bus and continue with their journey to Malawi.

However, this is a very risky venture and is not as easy and smooth as it sounds here. While walking passed the border they observe some precautions, for instance, they avoid to walk as a group, but have to walk singly; secondly, they have to surrender their bus tickets to the host or driver and upon interrogation by the authorities, they have to maintain that they are not on any bus. Otherwise, if the authorities discover this, they impound and detain the concerned bus hours on end, with other severe penalties, for example, a hefty fine, following thereafter. There are stories that such buses have sometimes been detained, say, for five hours at Beitbridge and only being released after settling the fine in question. Although in most cases such migrants end up crossing the border through this arrangement, they have untold problems when trying to enter South Africa when traveling from Malawi back to their work places in South Africa. For instance, they have to explain why their passports are missing some stamps (as a result of "border jumping") and they have to be ready to pay hefty bribes to be allowed entry.

Apart from migrants paying various bribes, as elucidated, there is also the tendency of drivers paying fines and bribes for the various offences. The traffic officers along the way literally behave like vultures, ready to pounce on public transport like buses. What I noted is that they also apply what one might call "selective justice", that is, they choose which buses to impound. As for established coaches like Intercape, their drivers are usually spared; they are not pestered like the drivers of small bus companies like Chipozani Coaches from Malawi. I personally travelled using each of these buses on separate occasions and the experience with traffic officers was radically different. With small bus companies, the traffic officers are literally seen to be fault-finding, to ensure the drivers pay a little bribe.

Traveling using Chipozani Coaches from South Africa on the way to Malawi, the journey was a nightmare. After traveling for about two hours from Johannesburg, the irritating stoppages started. At every police stop we spent an average of thirty minutes or one hour. We came to learn that these traffic officers not only in South Africa, but also in Zimbabwe and Mozambique, deliberately target the small buses and give their drivers a hell of trouble on the roads. While our bus used to be stopped, the other buses belonging to big companies merely passed through. This happened throughout our trip. After being stopped, we could only be released after the drivers parted with some money. The situation was even worse in Zimbabwe where these traffic officers usually demand bribes in dollars and not in any other currency. If it is to be in South African Rands, then it is the equivalent of what you are expected to pay in dollars. One can only imagine the overall impact this development had on the total travel period! Instead of one and half days, we took a whopping three days before we arrived in Malawi.

In Zimbabwe and in Mozambique the road blocks are so numerous, especially at night, that travel progress is virtually slowed down. Immediately after we started off at Zimbabwe Border Post after crossing Beitbridge, the traffic officers started stopping our bus every now and then. While this was happening, buses like Intercape used to overtake us one after another. After traveling for some three hours our drivers confessed that all the money that they had for eventualities had been used up and they were appealing to passengers to contribute a little something towards that cause if we were to catch up with our travel programme. At this point there was an uproar in the bus, with passengers refusing to be party to that kind of institutionalized corruption: "We cannot be party to that; we paid you money in line with the transport fare and that is sufficient. We are not supposed to contribute towards alleviating your vehicle problems along the way. That is your business, period", fumed the passengers aboard the coach. Passengers further maintained that they were ready to be delayed further, 'moreover, we have already wasted travel time'.

In a related development, a similar scenario was narrated by Tilipo, my friend who is based in South Africa, but travelled from Johannesburg to Malawi using his personal car. He was working in South Africa, but had decided to travel home with his entire family. He mainly encountered two great problems *en route* to Malawi: vehicle breakdowns and incessant requests for bribes from the traffic police. Although his car developed some technical faults along the way, it was the police bribes which proved more disturbing. By the time he reached Zimbabwe he got so furious with their incessant demands that he literally refused to cooperate. This was after his vehicle had already given him enough tough time with breakdowns: the vehicle was over-heating and the "bush mechanics" were of little help to him! They could hardly fix his vehicle; all they did was to extort some money from him. "I will not give you any money and if you insist that you will, therefore, not allow me to pass, then so be it. Moreover, I am already exhausted as I have been on the road for two whole days now", Tilipo 'charged' at a traffic police officer. At this point, he pulled his car over and slept! After some two hours of adequate sleep, the police officer woke him up and enquired: "Are you no longer continuing with your journey?" "I already told you that I don't have money left; all my money has been spent on trying to fix my vehicle and in giving bribes to your colleagues earlier on", explained Tilipo. At this point, he was released after paying R20 when initially the police officers were demanding R200!

Corruption between Traders and Border Officials

While labour migrants struggle a lot in trying to enter South Africa at Beitbridge, traders struggle a lot during the reverse trip, that is, on their way from South Africa to Malawi and especially at Mwanza and Dedza border posts. For these traders, it is when they are entering Malawi with a lot of trade goods bought in South Africa. During this trip, these traders have to clear these goods with Malawi Customs officers, by way of paying customs duty. Since they travel on a regular basis, the problem mainly faced by labour migrants, that is, of overstaying in South Africa, hardly applies to these traders. Hence after departure from Johannesburg, these traders unlike labour migrants, have a stress-free journey through all the border posts in South Africa, Zimbabwe and in Mozambique until they reach Malawi's borders in Mwanza and Dedza districts. In short, while labour migrants are responsible for all the delays in all the earlier borders, and most of all at Beitbridge, traders are responsible for the delays at the end of the two-day journeys: at Malawi's entry posts.

The largest proportion of Malawian traders plying their business between Malawi and South Africa are women. Although some Malawian labour migrants switch to various types of businesses after years of working in South Africa, most of these female traders are not former labour migrants; rather they are those who were doing business locally (within Malawi) and later, as part of their business growth or mere diversification, extend their business to South Africa. They mainly travel to South Africa to purchase *katundu* (goods) in bulk on wholesale price and later sell them at retail price to ensure profit in Malawi. They mainly deal in grocery items including soap, cooking oil and various kitchen ware; mens', women's and children's fashion clothes; and various school uniforms. Most of the female Malawian traders I interviewed indicated that school uniform is hot business and its demand has risen over the previous years in Malawi following the opening of many private schools. These uniforms are bought cheaply in South Africa and traders make huge profits out of them.

Most of these women operate mainly from the major cities of Lilongwe (Capital City), Blantyre (the major commercial city in Malawi), Zomba (the education hub of the country), and Mzuzu (the evergreen city in northern Malawi). Although Zomba is the newest of them all, there are many educational institutions at both secondary school and tertiary education level, hence school-related items like various stationery products are on very high demand in Zomba. Apart from Zomba, there is established market because of a strong buying power in the cities of Lilongwe and Blantyre. Most people in these cities have good jobs and businesses and therefore go with fashion or trend. Since most of the fashion ware is expensive in the local shops, a good number of people prefer giving orders to these female traders for them to buy in South Africa and supply them in Lilongwe and Blantyre at relatively better retail prices. Mzuzu, being the fastest growing city in the country, has a huge market potential for various items. Consequently, most traders have established businesses in various merchandise, for example, hardware items including paints, car parts, construction materials and household and office furnishings.

However, despite this huge market for various South African manufactured products, most traders do not have enough capital outlay. Their businesses rely on customers paying for the ordered items first. This implies these traders going to South Africa, buying goods using their limited and in most cases meagre financial resources and clearing these goods upon entry at Mwanza and Dedza border posts. This becomes an enormous and expensive undertaking by these traders. Consequently, in most cases they struggle to clear their *katundu* at the borders. Most of them indicated that they only manage to get some small bank loans as capital to buy these *katundu* in South Africa. They hardly get huge loans from banks because they do not have property to use as collateral in getting these loans and also because of the huge interest rates which limit someone to get huge loan amounts. The interest rates in various banks in Malawi hover around fifty per cent. In addition to this limiting factor, the loan repayment period is usually short, for instance, an average of one to two years, generally.

As a result of these developments and, in short, limited capital outlay, most Malawian traders resort to indulging in *vimbundi* or *katangale* (corrupt practices). They connive with various officers at the border posts for a mechanism to cut down on custom duty. Whereas labour migrants mainly bribe immigration officers for special favours, traders enter into shady deals with customs officers for reduced duty on their goods. This is done in various ways, one of these being under-declaring the value of goods bought in South Africa. For instance, a trader who has bought *katundu* worth R50,000 ends up declaring that his or her goods are worth only R25,000, hence under-declaring by fifty per cent. Consequently, while the concerned customs officer is fully aware of the actual value of these goods, he or she goes ahead calculating custom duty based on the declared figure of R25,000. Thereafter, the trader gives him or her a token of appreciation for such a favour. In this way, most traders spend far less on duty than is expected of them.

The other way is whereby these traders befriend some border officials, with some female traders indulging in sexual relationships with them. As a result, it is these officers-cum-boyfriends who are ready to ensure that these traders-cum-lovers get some special favours or treatment when entering with goods. Personal observation at Dedza Border showed that, indeed, some of these traders have such love affairs. When approaching the border, you find most of them making lengthy phone calls indulging in some intimate conversations with their "boyfriends" (literally man friends). It was learnt that some of these female traders would deliberately delay their departure from Johannesburg, South Africa, by a few days to make sure that they cross at a particular border when their friends are on duty. In this case, because of familiarity, even when their boyfriends are off-duty, the boyfriends' colleagues also do assist these traders in times of need.

The issue of familiarity is also exploited in various ways by these male and female traders. In some cases it is not love affairs which come into play, but mere friendships. Because these traders are frequent travellers, they befriend most of the customs officials and the latter are ready to give them some special treatment in exchange for some little token. The latter may either be in the form of part of the goods brought, for instance, giving the concerned officer, say two tins of milk, or giving him a little money, for instance, to the tune of R500 and paying duty of R12,000 instead of the official duty of R25,000. Again here personal observation at these borders revealed some of these traders giving customs officers a small proportion of their goods for their home use. Others could be seen making some phone calls informing the officer on duty to send one of the boys to the clearing scene to collect such goods for them.

In some cases, such *vimbundi* would come in the form of these custom officers sending these traders to buy goods for them in South Africa. Upon reaching the border, it is now the turn of these custom officers reciprocating such kind of a favour or good gesture by these traders. It so happens that since there are now two sets of *katundu*, the trader would declare say fifty per cent of his or her goods as belonging to the customs officer, who would not be harassed by fellow officers, as far as payment of duty is concerned. Through this arrangement, the trader is only required to pay duty on half of his or her *katundu* brought from South Africa. The other way is by packaging gimmick. When packing goods, they deliberately pack expensive goods together with less expensive or valued goods. For instance, laptops and other expensive electronic gadgets are packed inside blankets, duvets, clothes or school uniform. Now during clearing, the customs officers merely calculate goods based on the outer, less-expensive goods, hence arriving at less duty on the goods bought by a particular trader. In some cases, these officers are deliberately less strict in checking what is actually contained in the sealed package. This way, in the eyes of the onlookers, the officer would be seen to be doing his clearance job professionally, when in fact, it is a secret deal with the trader. After official duty is paid, the trader and officer pay each other tokens of appreciation behind the scenes, without anyone noticing or merely suspecting. These are but some of the many ways through which traders indulge in corrupt practices, all in the quest of making sure that duty is but 'halved'!

Photograph 4: Malawian labour migrants and traders are prone to accidents like this one *en route* between Malawi and South Africa. Of these two groups, it is traders' lives which are more at risk since they travel more frequently, for instance, once or twice every month. As for labour migrants, they take long, say, two or three years, before returning to Malawi (Source: social media; Facebook uploads).

Chapter Four

Of Migrants' and Traders' Stay in South Africa

Labour migrants and traders face untold problems during their journeys to and from South Africa as highlighted in chapters two and three. However, their stay in South Africa too is not without challenges. Their challenges border on basic survival: if the migrants have to fulfil their respective migration goals, they have to ensure an elongated and stress-free stay in South Africa. As for traders, since business is about making profits, they have to ensure that at the end of the day, they have made a significant profit margin. The latter will offset the costs incurred on transport to and from South Africa and also incurred during their brief stay in South Africa. In short, the labour migrants' and traders' scenario in South Africa, just like during their journeys to and from South Africa, can be equated to being between a rock and a hard place: whatever the case, both have to devise survival strategies. This chapter highlights some of the challenges that labour migrants and traders face during their stay in South Africa and the efforts they make in order to remain buoyant, that is, to remain on top of the survival game.

Malawian Migrants' Stay in South Africa

Labour migrants, especially *selufu* migrants, have been facing challenges during their stay in South Africa since time immemorial. During the old migration period, *selufu* migrants faced problems because their entry into South Africa was illegal. They entered South Africa illegally and after being discovered they were liable for repatriation back home. Even after serving for six months at *Bethani* Prison and after they were released they were still classified as unwanted or unauthorized migrants in South Africa. Hence they were not free to move about in towns. Consequently, they quickly made efforts to secure employment and virtually remained indoors thereafter. There are stories of such *selufu* migrants who made efforts to change their names, in the process adopting South African names. They also quickly learnt the local languages with the hope of quickly getting integrated into the South African society. It is some of these *selufu* migrants who ended up overstaying in South Africa.

In a desperate effort to survive in a 'turbulent' South Africa, some of these *selufu* migrants married local South African women and in so doing became part and parcel of the South African society. With time, they became bona fide South African citizens themselves, fully enjoying the privileges enjoyed by fellow South Africans, for example, access to jobs and pieces of land on which to build a house and settle. There are stories told by a number of former Malawian labour migrants that it was very easy for them to be accepted as South Africans through these marriages with local women. The latter, after becoming wives of Malawian *selufu* migrants, easily facilitated the process of securing the much-needed South African Identity Card (ID) for their husbands. After securing such IDs, *selufu* migrants, then with the status of a South African citizen, easily moved around in towns without any form of harassment by the police and immigration authorities.

In 2016 in Deipsloot shanty location in Johannesburg, South Africa, I met Vyamucharo, a Malawian from the central region of Dedza in Malawi, who narrated that he first came to South Africa in the 1960s initially as a *Wenela* migrant and after working in various mines he returned to Malawi. Afterwards he came back as a *selufu* migrant and started working in various sectors. He worked as a domestic worker and later on secured work in a company. Here he worked till he retired and got his benefits. When he came as a *selufu* migrant, he got married to a local South African woman as a strategy to gain acceptance in society. He had seven children with this wife. However, all these years he had been in South Africa, he maintained ties with his people at home in Malawi. He did this by visiting his home at least once every two years. By the time I was interviewing him in 2016 he still had strong links with his home people in Dedza District, Malawi. After he retired, he secured plots in Diepsloot and constructed small houses for rent and transformed himself into a small-scale businessman, owning rented property. "Although I am not working, I am doing fine and I have all the hope that this situation will continue into the future; all this is a result of the investments I made into rented property using my retirement package", claimed Vyamucharo.

In a related development, in October 2015 in a bus from Malawi to South Africa, I travelled together with Mutende, a former labour migrant from Mzimba District. Just like Vyamucharo, Mutende had worked in various mines under the auspices of *Wenela*. After these *Wenela* contracts, he secured different jobs as a *selufu* migrant. It is also during this period that Mutende married a local South African woman. He too had children with this local wife. However, despite such developments in South Africa, he still maintained his Malawian wife, with whom he also had children. He was polygamous, with two wives: one based at his home village in Malawi and the other one, South African, in South Africa. From my conversation with him, his first wife in Malawi was fully aware that he had a second wife in South Africa. Similarly, the wife in South Africa knew Mutende was married with children in Malawi. Hence the South African wife was not surprised with her husband's regular visits to Malawi. After he retired, he relocated to his home village in Mzimba District, Malawi. However, he continued to visit his wife and children in Honeydew, South Africa, at least once every six months. He also had developed old age complications, like blood pressure, and, therefore, travelled to South Africa from time to time to access better medical attention in South African hospitals. In fact, this was his aim for going to South Africa in October 2015.

The third case is that of Panganani, a *selufu* migrant from Chintcheche in Nkhata-Bay District, who first went to South Africa in the 1950s. Like the majority of migrants from the district, Panganani went to South Africa as a *selufu* migrant. However, he is one of the few *selufu* migrants who eventually ended up working in the mines in the quest of getting better wages. He too married a South African woman and they had children together. Luckily, his children managed to attain education and secured good-paying jobs, thereafter. Despite securing a South Africa ID and getting integrated into the South African society, after staying in South Africa for half a century, he impressed on his children on the need for him to return to his ancestral home in Malawi and to die and be buried amongst his kinsmen. His children obliged and formally escorted their elderly father back to Nkhata-Bay, Malawi. Thereafter, it was his children who started paying him regular visits in Malawi alongside bringing different forms of assistance.

These are but some of the numerous cases of Malawian *selufu* migrants making efforts to integrate into the South African society through inter-marriages during the old migration period. Although some of these migrants told their Malawian wives about the second wives in South Africa, others kept it as a secret throughout their married lives. This was done to avoid their marriages from collapsing as some Malawian wives were against being in a polygamous family. After learning about this polygamy, such wives simply opted out of such marriages; and went back to their original villages or simply got married to other Malawian men within Malawi.

However, some Malawian women from patriarchal societies, though rare, openly declared that they did not mind whether their husband had another wife in South Africa or not. What mattered to them was whether or not their husband was looking after the welfare of their household: sending financial assistance from South Africa for their daily subsistence back home, for farming and for their children's education needs. "If my husband really wants to indulge in extra-marital affairs I cannot control him whether he is based here or in South Africa. But what is of importance to me is for my husband not to abandon me and the children: If he continues to fend for our needs, then I have no problems whatsoever since he is free and has his own life to live!" Said Pilirani, a wife to a labour migrant who had another wife in South Africa. Personal observation at their home in Mzimba District in Malawi showed that they were doing fine. They had invested part of the proceeds from South Africa in farming and they had also opened a grocery shop. It was Pilirani, the wife, who was running this shop while the husband continued working in South Africa.

During the new migration period, most male and female labour migrants continued to face numerous challenges. These challenges mainly had to do with accommodation and food challenges; job scarcity; excessive beer drinking; collapse of marriages; xenophobia and arrests and deportations. One of the most immediate challenges that labour migrants face in South Africa border on finding accommodation and food. This becomes a serious problem before one secures a job. Most of them arrive at their relatives' residential places and only move to their own premises after securing some kind of jobs. The latter may initially be temporary and they secure more permanent and better-paying jobs with time. However, there are some scenarios where some labour migrants either do not have relatives already working in South Africa or they have relatives quite alright, but their relatives' circumstances do not permit them to host their incoming migrant relatives. For instance, some employers do not allow their domestic workers to host their relatives in their servants' quarters. This creates a difficult situation for labour migrants who have just arrived from Malawi and are yet to secure own jobs.

In extreme cases, some of these migrants, especially female labour migrants, are compelled to resort to some unusual measures in order to ensure survival. During this period they lack almost everything: food and accommodation. Out of desperation, there are scenarios where some female labour migrants have resorted to cohabiting with fellow established Malawian male migrants, in the process entering "marriages of convenience". Most of these Malawian female migrants are "single women" like divorcees and widows who go to South Africa to look for wage employment in a bid to secure money with which to look after their children. After the collapse of their marriages and the deaths of their husbands, some of whom were former labour migrants, these women take emigrating and working in South Africa as a last resort. Despite such accommodation challenges, they are ready to hang on in order to eventually secure such jobs. During my oral interviews with such female migrants, a few of them openly said that, indeed, they entered such informal marriages in order to survive. But while in such marriages, they made it clear to the husband that they were in South Africa to work, accumulate money, and thereafter return to their children in Malawi. Their husbands had no problems with such an arrangement since, they, too, were already married and had children, hence family responsibility, in Malawi.

In Diepsloot in 2016 I came across Tiyezge, a Malawian female migrant who was in an informal affair with a Malawian male migrant, who was already married and with children in Malawi. Tiyezge decided to go to South Africa after the death of her husband. Before the death of her husband, Tiyezge was doing small-scale businesses using proceeds from her husband's job. They had three children together and Tiyezge had problems looking after her children after the death of her husband. Her main wish was to be self-reliant and to train all her three children. However, her small business could not support her children's expensive fees and other needs. That is when she decided to emigrate and work in South Africa. Upon arrival, her relatives assisted her in securing a stable job as a domestic worker. She was happily employed, but eventually entered into an affair with a fellow Malawian male migrant worker for the sake of conjugal rights.

Despite this arrangement, Tiyezge continued staying at her employer's compound and only visited her boyfriend from time to time. Again this did not distract her from her goal: she continued sending money and other forms of assistance, like clothes and shoes, to her children back home. By the time of the interview, one of her three children had started secondary school education and she was able to pay for his school fees at a private secondary school. Apart from school fees, Tiyezge had managed to build a three-bedroom house which she was renting out; she had also bought a plot which she planned to develop in the near future. Such investments in rented property were part of her preparation for life after years of working in South Africa. She was fully aware that once back home, she needed a stable source of money since she would no longer be working. Hence she had to make sound investments "while the sun was still shining". She indicated she had plans of staying three more years in South Africa before finally returning back home. "I need to be with my children more now that they are in secondary school. They need my constant encouragement and support now if they are to perform well at the end of their secondary school education. Without my presence, the children may end up going astray because of lack of parental guidance and control", argued Tiyezge.

While most households decide to send one member, usually a father, to South Africa for wage employment as a solution to the financial hardships a family is facing, going to South Africa is associated with the introduction of fresh problems in most migrant households back home. In cases where the husband leaves the wife and children back home and ends up working in South Africa, the husband at times ends up abandoning his family in favour of other women in South Africa. Thus labour migration is a source of marriage break-ups and divorces. This is a sad development because instead of merely solving the said financial problems within the household, other more serious problems result. Consequently, a number of women have regretted allowing their husbands to go to South Africa in the first place, arguing "although we were facing financial problems, we used to stay as husband and wife and looked after our children together".

The other problem with having secret affairs in South Africa is that with time a husband stops sending assistance to the wife back home, with the wife thereafter struggling to fend for the children and the entire household. Such a development has in some situations forced the wife back home to also indulge in extra-marital affairs without the knowledge of the husband who is based in South Africa. This has resulted in the partners contracting sexually transmitted diseases and thereafter infecting each other. This trend has been happening for so many years since the old migration period. While in the past, the common STDs were *chindoko* and *chizonono* (syphilis and gonorrhoea), in the new migration period these STDs include HIV which leads to AIDS. A visit to most of the major labour migration areas in Malawi shows that many houses are deserted, with either a partner or both husband and wife having died of these STDs. This is one of the reasons why most migrant husbands nowadays aim at working briefly in South Africa, say, for three to five years before returning back home for good in order to be with their wives and children. This trend contrasts sharply with the old practice of migrant husbands taking wage employment in South Africa as a form of occupation.

In addition to husbands abandoning their wives back in Malawi as a result of getting new South African women, of late there is a new trend involving female migrants dumping their husbands right in South Africa. Since the early 1990s different categories of women joined the labour migration scene. Initially it was wives of migrant husbands visiting them in South Africa for brief periods, for instance, for three months. Later on, even single women including divorcees and widows joined the labour migration scene. These female migrants started feeling bossy towards their husbands after securing jobs, mostly as domestic servants. The exposure in South Africa and the wages from their employment "entered their heads" and they started thinking "we can as well stand on our own without due help from our husbands". Most of them stopped being submissive to their husbands, shouting at their husbands amidst declaring "I don't need you by my side. In fact, I can as well stand on my own!"

There are a lot of stories of such female migrants (just like male migrants) indulging in extra-marital affairs right in South Africa without fear of being discovered by their husbands. In case the husband comes to know, the wife is ready to stand alone, in the end resulting in the collapse of their marriage. Such developments also result after the husband loses his job for one reason or another, for instance, following arrests and deportations. Once the husband is deported, he loses his job in the process and by the time he goes back to South Africa, the wife has a boyfriend who is equally working. Since the husband is not working, hence regarded as excess baggage, his wife prefers continuing with the boyfriend at the expense of her rightful husband right in South Africa and their children back in Malawi.

In 2015 I met Tambulani, a male migrant whose wife dumped him in favour of a Malawian boyfriend also working in South Africa. He narrated that he had first gone to South Africa about ten years ago. While working there, he used to get annual holidays during which he usually visited his wife and children in Malawi. After working for a couple of years, he decided to invite his wife for a short visit in South Africa. "I wanted my wife to see South Africa", said Tambulani. Indeed, the wife paid him a visit one year. She stayed in South Africa for three months and returned to Malawi. During one of his visits to Malawi, his wife requested him to allow the wife to join him in South Africa, this time not for a mere visit but with the aim of equally looking for a temporary job. The reasoning behind this was that it was better for both of them to work as they would, in this way, easily meet their household migration goals. Tambulani saw sense in this thinking and obliged. The following year he invited the wife to South Africa. He also asked his boss for an employment opportunity for his wife. Luckily, the boss offered his wife a job as a domestic worker and they lived happily together.

However, one day disaster struck: Tambulani was arrested by the police in the company of his friends from Zimbabwe. They were later taken to Lindela Repatriation Centre and were eventually deported. Since he took some three months to organize his trip back to South Africa, he lost his job in the process. His boss replaced him with another migrant worker. This meant he became jobless. Unfortunately, he had problems finding a replacement job. It was during this period when his wife started becoming unruly and uncooperative. After a few months his friends told him that his wife had found a boyfriend during the three months he spent in Malawi following his deportation. He could not believe his ears, but eventually he proved his friends right: his wife, indeed, had a boyfriend. He tried to talk to his wife to refrain from such extra-marital affairs, but to no avail. "My wife openly told me she could not cope staying with a husband who was jobless, arguing the husband is supposed to take care of his wife and children and not otherwise", complained Tambulani. Afterwards, the wife actually declared their marriage over and continued going out with her boyfriend. Tambulani was shocked and regretted: "The only crime that I committed was to allow my wife to join me in South Africa in order to look for a job. I wish my wife remained in Malawi, in line with our earlier arrangement", said

Tambulani. Tambulani's scenario is one of the numerous sad stories surrounding Malawian male labour migrants whose marriages collapse after allowing their wives to equally work in South Africa in the quest of accumulating more proceeds.

Malawian Traders' Stay in South Africa

Unlike labour migrants who face numerous problems in South Africa since they stay longer and in most cases for many years, traders stay briefly, usually from a few days to a few weeks before returning to Malawi, and, therefore, do not face many problems during this brief stay. The most important solace on their part is that they do not overstay in South Africa: they return to Malawi, having bought *katundu* for resale, before the expiry of the allocated 30-day visas. Consequently, they do not usually have problems with the police and Home Affairs officials in South Africa. They freely move about, purchasing their trade items. In spite of this development, their stay in South Africa is not wholly stress-free.

Traders' obsession is to maximize on the profits from the sale of South African goods in Malawi. Hence during their stay in South Africa, though already brief, they make strenuous efforts to spend less on accommodation and meals and save some money which they use on buying goods at wholesale prices. The thinking behind this is the more the goods bought, the higher the profits back in Malawi. Consequently, they devise strategies on how to cut down on costs. One way is going for cheaper meals and avoiding expensive lodges in favour of cheaper and more affordable guest houses. A visit to one of the popular lodging places of these traders in Johannesburg revealed that the traders lodge in sub-standard and filthy places, all in the name of ensuring some savings.

Even their usual eating places are sub-standard and a health hazard. These places are within the vicinity of the departure points of such coaches like Chipozani Coaches. This is deliberately done to ensure that they avoid transport costs, for instance, hiring taxis to the departure points. Since they buy a lot of goods, staying away from these departure points would mean incurring huge expenses in transporting these trade items to the coaches for onward loading just before departing for Malawi.

Another strategy, which is not different from the one espoused by female labour migrants, is finding boyfriends in South Africa. For traders, the intention is to make sure these boyfriends or lovers subsidize their expenses during their brief stay in South Africa. The boyfriends are, therefore, in charge over accommodation and meals' costs during each of their visits in South Africa. In such a way, the traders do save some money as their money is exclusively used as capital to buy goods on wholesale for resale in Malawi. Personal observations aboard the buses from Malawi to South Africa revealed that these traders are always making phone calls alerting these boyfriends about the arrival time in Johannesburg so that they should come to pick them up. For some, they literally spend the entire shopping days at the place of their boyfriends. This way, they avoid costs for meals and accommodation as these are fully taken care of by these boyfriends.

In some instances, these lovers are not based in South Africa, but in Malawi. Hence they provide such subsidies before departure in Malawi. There are stories of boyfriends contributing towards travel and accommodation expenses during such shopping trips. In some cases, these traders actually look for top-ups on their capital outlay. In this way, the traders end up buying a lot of goods, hence more profits.

It has also been indicated that some of these traders have multiple boyfriends with the aim of maximizing on money for this capital. With a number of boyfriends, it is rare that all of them provide top-ups at the same time. But assuming one has three boyfriends, the likelihood that at least one or two of them will provide some supplementary money during a particular trip is high.

It is, therefore, not a surprise that most traders are regarded as having loose morals since they are obsessed with making or finding money to top-up on their business capital. There are stories of some of these women indulging in elements of prostitution both in Malawi and South Africa in order to make additional money. This is on top of the money realized from profits in their businesses. I personally heard some female traders aboard some coaches on the way from Johannesburg to Malawi chatting and one of them saying "I was very lucky this time I met a partner with a lot of money. He took me out for beers and afterwards also gave me a lot of money to top-up on my capital". This was merely a modest way of saying that she actually indulged in prostitution, that is, offering her body in exchange for money.

It is shocking to learn that some of these women are actually married, with husbands and children in Malawi. They get capital from their working husbands in order to venture into some cross-border business. However, without their husbands and relatives knowing, while in South Africa they combine business with prostitution. For some ladies, they spend a week buying merchandise in South Africa, but end up staying for a total of three weeks in South Africa. They spend the remaining two weeks in brothels in South Africa, accumulating additional capital. As a cover, they feed their husbands with lies, for instance, that they had a breakdown on the way to South Africa and, therefore, took more days to arrive. If not, they report that they will take longer in South Africa since they have problems buying South African Rands at affordable rates or that the goods are very expensive and they are, therefore, going places looking for cheaper outlets. These are some of the many gimmicks employed by Malawian traders in South Africa as they make efforts to maximize on their capital for their respective businesses. Because of this image that they have back home, some husbands virtually do not allow their wives to indulge in cross-border trade.

Photograph 5: Malawian labour migrants being dispersed by South African police at Randburg Park, Johannesburg, in November 2016 on grounds that they did not seek permission from the relevant authorities. However, the migrants maintained this was mere routine harassment by the police against foreign nationals. This was around 12:30 p.m. (noon) and, according to the police, everyone was expected to have left by 1:00 p.m. I was in the middle of conducting oral interviews with Malawian migrants as part of my research and we had to hurriedly leave, running for our dear lives! (photo by author).

Chapter Five

Of Malawian Culture Abroad

In the history of labour migration from Malawi to countries in the southern Africa region, a lot has been written on how Malawian labour migrants came under the influence of foreign cultures. Labour migrants returning from the mines in South Africa brought the South African culture to Malawi. This chapter examines the flip-side of the coin: how years of migration to South Africa and other countries in the region, for example, Zambia and Zimbabwe, led to the exportation of Malawian culture abroad. These aspects of Malawian culture include language, dressing and traditional dances or cultural practices. This chapter, therefore, fervently argues and shows that, though a minority in these destination countries, Malawians over the years have come to have a lasting cultural impression on the people, who are in a clear-cut majority, in these destination countries.

Malawian migrants returning from countries in southern Africa brought home different aspects of foreign culture. After being away for a number of years, the people in Malawi regarded these migrant returnees highly and considered whatever cultural aspect they brought as advanced. They, therefore, made efforts to adopt the new culture. For instance, returning migrants spoke and introduced foreign languages in Malawi. These included various local languages spoken in the destination countries including English. The people back in Malawi were keen to learn and speak these new languages. With the passage of time, this led to what I might call the hybridization of local languages in that the local languages eventually took on board various foreign words which became 'naturalised'.

They also brought new forms of dressing and this included both clothes and shoes. In the 1980s what became popular were high-heeled 'massive' shoes popularly and colloquially known as '*chiphwanya mchenga*' (literally the destroyer of sand) in Chitumbuka language of northern Malawi. They also popularized long and flared trousers (*mafuleya*) and dresses (*jojeti*). These became a darling among many people and almost everyone wished they owned such clothes and shoes. Men returning from South Africa usually brought home jackets and hats usually made from leather. This is the trend even up to the present. If they are to bring home gifts to their loved ones, for instance, wives, children and other relatives, they made a point to include some of these clothes since they were highly valued and hence the recipients appreciated receiving such gifts.

Although beer drinking is part and parcel of the culture of the Ngoni of Mzimba and Ntcheu-Dedza areas in Malawi, the returning migrants were seen to be indulging in excessive beer drinking and womanizing habits. This, as highlighted elsewhere in this book, led to the virtual collapse of some of the marriages of these migrant labourers. The Ngoni are culturally polygamous and, upon return, the migrants were usually marrying another wife. This also brought about disharmony in the household. A few of these migrants brought home their South African wives. However, in most cases the latter failed to adapt to a tough village life in rural Malawi and eventually simply went back to South Africa.

In addition, foreign culture has had a lasting impact in Malawi within the entertainment circles. Although Malawians are good at music, the dominant themes in their music is suffering and sorrow, reflecting the general plight in society.

For instance, most musicians sing about poverty, hunger and disease and how Malawians may escape this suffering. No wonder, most of the songs also have religious and gospel messages since the poor usually tend to put their hope in God. One of the Malawian musicians in this case is Lawrence Mbenjere of the *chiphaso* (passport) fame who bemoans the economic hardships in Malawi and in one of his songs he wishes he possessed a passport which would have enabled him to go to South Africa for wage employment. This was a sharp contrast from the music which was introduced by the returning migrant workers, especially from Zimbabwe and South Africa. This was music whose main theme was merry making: to show that one is happy. Consequently, most people embraced this type of music as a viable alternative. In fact, Zimbabwean and South African music became very popular in Malawi. Growing up in the northern districts of Mzimba, Rumphi and Nkhata-Bay in the 1980s and 1990s, I personally witnessed the boom and popularization of such music. The music in question was played during *mthimba* (wedding ceremony), drinking places and during festive seasons like Christmas. After harvest period, women usually brew local beer using *lipoko* (millet). This beer is usually for sale and between July and November, ahead of the next growing season, there is a lot of merry making since people do not go to their gardens.

The returning migrants had a tendency of bringing home *Magumbagumba* (musical equipment) which they were using during such occasions. With time, there was also the practice of offering this equipment for hire and it was being used during ceremonies like weddings. Through this, the equipment owner was getting paid afterwards. Even nowadays South African and Zimbabwean music is still very popular in northern Malawi. Selected songs by popular musicians of South Africa and

Zimbabwe origin still enjoy 'air space' in popular bars and bottle stores across the country.

On the export of Malawian cultures abroad some writers have documented how the Chewa migrants from central Malawi have introduced *gulewamkulu* ("the big dance") and *nyau* secret societies in Zimbabwe. *Gulewamkulu* is a traditional dance under the *nyau* societies and has been popular for a long time among the Chewa in Malawi and parts of Zambia. It is associated with secrecy and only men are actively involved. In fact, not every man in society is an automatic member of *nyau*. One has to be initiated first and once a member, one is not supposed to divulge secrets to non-members. In their original form, *nyau* activities take place in the grave yards or in places which are secluded from the society. This is why people associate *nyau* societies with elements of witchcraft. In fact, there are some stories which state that once one reveals what happens in these *nyau* societies to the 'outside world', he is bound to die as a form of punishment.

With the passage of time, *gulewamkulu* started being featured during every-day ceremonies and *nyau* was no longer a secret cult as it used to be. For instance, it was a regular feature during political and social functions in Malawi. It was during this period when Malawians emigrating to Zimbabwe introduced *nyau* and *gulewamkulu* in their midst right in the destination areas. Nowadays, it remains a popular and not-so-secret dance not only in Malawi, but also in Zimbabwe. In the pre-1990 period, children in Malawi used to run for safety whenever *gulewamkulu* dancers were approaching. These days that is a thing of the past. While in the past, the *gulewamkulu* dancers were regarded as *vilombo* (spirits), nowadays you would overhear children arguing amongst themselves that "those are not spirits, but real people merely putting on masks". In fact, these days even the masks in question are not professionally done, revealing part of one's body, for instance, hands and feet.

Malawians have many languages in line with their ethnic groupings. However, there are about four main ethnic groups and these are Chewa, Tumbuka, Yao and Lhomwe. Hence the major local languages are Chichewa, Chitumbuka, Chiyao and Chilhomwe. Dr. Hastings Kamuzu Banda, the first president of independent Malawi (1964-1994), made Chichewa the official local language. In so doing, he promoted Chichewa over and above other local languages so much so that it is one of the languages taught in primary and secondary schools across the country. Consequently, almost every Malawian is expected to know and speak Chichewa. To make matters worse, in some instances, knowing and speaking Chichewa is regarded as a status symbol, just like speaking English.

Consequently, Malawian migrants have exported Chichewa language to various destination countries like Zimbabwe and South Africa. As for Zambia, the people speak Chinyanja which is more similar than different from Chichewa spoken in Malawi. Whoever you meet in South Africa and learns that you are from Malawi will greet you "*Achimwene, muli bwanji?*" (Brother, how are you?) This is enough proof of the influence and impact that Chichewa has had in other countries. And because of the long history of Malawian labour migration to Zimbabwe, and because of many Malawians who overstayed there and never returned, and also because of others who intermarried with the local Zimbabwean women there, there are, reportedly, whole communities in Zimbabwe which are conversant in Chichewa from Malawi. When you meet some immigrants from Zimbabwe in South Africa and they happen to have interacted with Malawians in Zimbabwe, you are amazed at the level of fluency in Chichewa. But upon inquiry, you discover they are not from Malawi or Zambia, where Chichewa and Chinyanja are spoken, rather they are from Bulawayo, Harare or any other town in Zimbabwe!

Apart from Chichewa, Malawian labour migrants have exported Chitumbuka, the dominant language in northern Malawi. Labour migration from Mzimba and Nkhata-Bay districts dates back to as early as the late 19th and early 20th centuries. It was the Tonga from Nkhata-Bay who were pioneers in this migration. In South Africa they usually sought wage employment in the gold mines. However, later they were joined by the Ngoni from Mzimba District. With time the Ngoni took emigration to South Africa seriously and managed to overtake the Tonga as far as dominance was concerned. Since the Ngoni overlords were culturally dominated by their Tumbuka subjects, Chitumbuka language became dominant among the Ngoni of Mzimba, replacing Chingoni, the Ngoni language. In fact, with time, Chitumbuka of the Tumbuka people from Rumphi, a district to the north of Mzimba, eventually spread and became dominant in the whole of the northern region.

Since the Ngoni, too, started emigrating to South Africa as part of their migrant tradition, and the fact that they tended to emigrate in large numbers, they eventually started exporting Chitumbuka to the respective destination areas in South Africa. The other factor behind the rapid spread of Chitumbuka was the system of migrant networks. The migrants from a particular household ended up facilitating the eventual emigration of other household members. In the destination areas, these migrants, who were either closely or distantly related, tended to stay in one area. Here the dominant language of communication continued to be Chitumbuka. Consequently, it so happened that the local South Africans gradually started learning Chitumbuka language of the immigrants in their midst: the Ngoni and Tumbuka from northern Malawi.

With time jobs became scarce in South Africa, especially following the influx of more immigrants from countries with faltering economies, for instance, Malawi, Zimbabwe and Mozambique. As a result of this, labour migrants could hardly secure long-term employment. Alternatively, they started relying on *maganyu*. However, the latter were not as reliable and high-paying. Consequently, these migrant workers were relegated to the shanty locations where accommodation was relatively cheaper. It is in these locations where the immigrants stayed side by side with local South Africans and immigrants from other countries. Where Malawian migrants inadvertently became dominant, they imparted Chitumbuka on their neighbours. It is reported that there are some locations in South Africa where the dominant language of communication is Chitumbuka of northern Malawi. This is because of the large numbers of migrant workers of Malawi origin.

In southern Malawi, the Yao also have a long history of working abroad. However, while the Ngoni of Mzimba and the Tonga of Nkhata-Bay prefer working as gardeners, cooks and house-keepers, the Yao from such districts as Mangochi, Machinga, Zomba and Balaka prefer to secure employment as shop assistants. This is because of their orientation and background. The Yao originated from parts of northern Mozambique and they were traders. They came to Malawi where they continued with this entrepreneurial spirit. In fact, the goal of most of the Yao is to start small-scale businesses in Malawi. While in South Africa, they work as shop assistants and in the process accumulate capital with which they start businesses in Malawi. In South Africa, these Yao are, indeed, found selling various merchandise belonging to Indians, the Chinese and, of late, Nigerians. However, there are a few Yaos who own their own businesses. In short, the Yao too have their own influence in terms of Chiyao language in the areas where they work and stay.

Apart from language, Malawian migrants also bring along other aspects of their culture like traditional dances and dressing. In South Africa, women are popularly known for their long dresses and special Malawian wrappers called *vitenje*. Whenever, you go around the streets of Johannesburg, you are able to recognise Malawians by the kind of dress. Unlike South African ladies, who usually put on short dresses and mini-skirts, their Malawian counter-parts put on long 'respectable' dresses. In fact, traditionally, in Malawi a lady who puts on very short dresses, especially in the countryside, is regarded as having loose morals: such women are regarded to be prostitutes, 'gallivanting' with men. In fact, you usually find people commenting that "look at her, she dressed like a prostitute", or "that kind of dressing belongs to the bottle stores and bars!"

There are stories of a town in Malawi where young men came up with an underground movement to rid the town of indecent dressing. Everyday they do their daily businesses, for instance, selling various merchandise, pushing wheelbarrows, operating *sakaramento* (bicycle taxis) and other activities, but while doing all this, everybody is patronizing the town. Whenever one of them spots a lady who is not properly dressed, he whistles in trying to draw the attention of his 'peers'. When this happens, hell breaks loose: within a few minutes almost all the men descend on the lady, literally stripping her of her clothes, arguing "since you didn't want to dress properly, like the Malawian way, why can't you just be completely naked!" They remove all her clothes, including the pants, and parade her naked around the city. They chant "this should be a lesson to all other women! Dress properly or don't dare come to town almost naked". Thereafter, they release her, without clothes, and chase her out of the town. The crowd is so large that even the police can hardly do anything.

On traditional dances, in Malawi all ethnic groups have their own respective traditional dances. For instance, the Ngoni of Mzimba are popular for *ingoma* and *mganda* dances; the Tonga for *malipenga*, the Chewa for *gulewamkulu* (as highlighted earlier in this chapter), *njedza*, *chisamba*, and *chimtali*; the Yao for *manganje*, *beni* and *tchopa*; the Lhomwe for *manganje*, tchopa and *masewe*; the Tumbuka for *vimbuza* and *malipenga*; and, lastly, the Nkhonde for *ndingala*, *malipenga* and *ulumba*. When the Ngoni and Tumbuka from Mzimba and Rumphi districts emigrate, they export such cultural aspects. A good number of the migrants from Mzimba District end up working in hotels and lodges in South Africa as cooks or chefs and waiters. Whenever there are a number of them at one place, they introduce some of these traditional dances as one way of entertaining guests at these lodges.

This is exactly what happens at Mangwa Valley Lodge, north of Johannesburg. I visited this place in 2016 and there were about five Malawian migrants working in different capacities at this place. When guests are staying for a number of days, on the eve of departure management of the lodge organizes a farewell dinner function in the evening. They light fire and food is served around the fire place. When people are having dinner, there are farewell speeches, with drum beating in the background. They randomly choose participants from the group and try to teach them how to beat these drums. This is accompanied by a brief presentation about the origin and nature of such traditional dances in their home districts in Malawi. In this way, these migrant workers are acting as "Goodwill Ambassadors" in the spread and popularization of Malawian culture abroad.

Photograph 6: Malawians working at Mangwa Valley Lodge, north of Johannesburg, singing and beating drums (Malawian culture) to entertain guests during an evening function around a fire place (photo by author).

Photograph 7: *Gulewamkulu* dancers, part of the *nyau* secret societies from the central region in Malawi

(Source: http://exploremalawi.blogspot.com/2012/07/great-dance-gule-wamkulu.html)

Chapter Six

The Failed Role of the State

The Malawi government has a role to play in ensuring that its migrant citizens' rights and general welfare are protected and enhanced in the destination countries, viz: Tanzania, South Africa and Zimbabwe. Although Malawian migrants are found in a number of other countries other than these, the highlighted countries feature as major destination countries for unskilled and semi-skilled migrants. The latter become vulnerable in the destination countries since they do not have immediate protection from different forms of harassment. During the old migration period in Malawi's history, that is, during the period up to the 1980s, the government was keenly involved in protecting the lives of its migrant citizens, especially in Zimbabwe and South Africa. However, during the new period, that is, in the post-1990 period, the government's support is but lukewarm and in most cases the government is seen to be reactive and not proactive. This chapter argues that the government needs to be concerned with the welfare of its migrant citizens even during the post-1990 period when migration is exclusively informal. It also highlights some latest initiatives taken by some Malawian migrants based in South Africa in trying to enhance the living standards of fellow Malawian migrants in South Africa.

During the old migration period, Malawi government was involved in inter-state negotiations with the governments of South Africa and Zimbabwe over the welfare of Malawian labour migrants working in those countries, that is, in the mines and farms, respectively. The government negotiated with Zimbabwe through *Mthandizi*, a body that was charged with the task of recruiting labour in Malawi for the Zimbabwean farms. As for South Africa, these negotiations were channelled through *Wenela* and later *Theba* on behalf of the South African Chamber of Mines, specifically, and the South African government, generally. Such negotiations touched on the improvement of general working conditions, for example, minimizing health risks in the mines and mine compounds. In addition, the government fought for better wages for its migrant citizens since better wages meant better foreign income. There was an arrangement whereby part of the labour migrants' wages ended up going into Malawi government coffers. In this case, the government was a direct beneficiary in terms of foreign exchange earnings. That is why the government, through the ministry of labour, was in the forefront fighting for improved working conditions in the South African mines and Zimbabwean farms.

However, this keen interest and direct involvement by the government ended with the collapse of mine migrancy at the end of the 1980s following the 1987 HIV dispute between Malawi and South Africa. Although Malawians continued to go to South Africa during the post-1990 period, they go there informally, that is, as *selufu* migrants. Consequently, since they largely work in the informal sector, the Malawi government is not directly involved in their welfare. However, it is during this period that large numbers of male and female labour migrants and traders flock to South Africa either for wage employment or for business purposes. Consequently, this lack of government intervention is the source of the many challenges that these labour migrants and traders face in South Africa.

For example, Malawian migrants are expected to bring along R3,000 when entering South Africa and yet immigrants from other countries like Zimbabwe and Mozambique are not required to bring this entry fee. The justification for this entry fee is that the money is used in case there is an abrupt need for the migrant to return to Malawi. However, this fee is a stumbling block when migrants are preparing to depart for South Africa. In addition to fetching transport money and money for the processing of the passport, these potential migrants have to fetch money equivalent to R3,000 as entry fee. This becomes an uphill task for rural dwellers and is the reason as to why *vimbundi* (corruption) is on the increase, especially, at Beitbridge Border Post and also why many potential migrants residing in Malawi's countryside fail to make it to South Africa. If the government was involved it could have negotiated either for the reduction of this fee or for its complete waiver, in line with what is happening with migrants from Zimbabwe and Mozambique.

Malawian migrants, together with migrants from other African countries, face a lot of problems during their stay in South Africa. One of the major problems since May 2008 is xenophobia. Although there have so far been two major waves of xenophobia in South Africa (May-June 2008 and April 2015), migrants have been facing subtle forms of xenophobia since the early 1990s, especially following the demise of apartheid and the consequent introduction of democratic governance in 1994. Most of these migrants residing in high residential areas like Diepsloot, Honeydew and Alexandra have been subjected to hatred by the South African locals on the grounds that these foreigners are responsible for various ills in society, for instance, scarcity of jobs, snatching of South African women and high crime rate, among others. They are, therefore, targeted with the express aim of evicting and forcing them back to their origin countries. Due to such hatred, a number of foreign workers have been attacked, with some actually being killed in the process. Others have had their household property looted and burnt.

Since a number of these foreigners are enterprising, they own grocery and hardware shops within these residential areas and also in some small trading centres and townships. As a result of this enterprising spirit, there is also an outcry amongst the South African locals who argue that their businesses fail to grow because of unfair competition from these foreign business men and women. During these waves of xenophobia, these migrants' shops are looted and pillaged. But what is perturbing is that after such looting and destruction of shops belonging to foreigners, the local South Africans do not come in to establish their small-scale businesses in these premises vacated by the entrepreneurial foreign traders. This simply leaves a lot to be desired and merely proves the commonplace sentiments that South Africans are not doing fine not because of undue competition from foreigners, but rather because of sheer laziness and a handouts syndrome. They are used to getting handouts including monthly subsidies from their government. As a consequence of this syndrome, they hate foreigners who usually make ends meet through a hard working spirit and dedication to duty.

In terms of jobs, it is partly because of this hard working spirit that most employers prefer foreign workers. They are also trustworthy at the work place. Since local South Africans want quick money, they are associated with pilfering at the work place. Consequently, they end up losing jobs not long after securing them. A number of Malawian migrants I interacted with were in agreement with the fact that Malawian migrant workers have a long history and good legacy of being hard working and trustworthy at the work place. In this connection, Tiwonge had this to say on the matter:

Ise tabanthu ba ku Malawi kuno mabwana ghakutitemwa chomene chifukwa chakulimbikira ntchito. Nangauli mazuba ghano ntchito zakusuzga kuzisanga, ise tikusuzgika chomene yayi chifukwa kuyambira kale bazigogo bithu balikuleka mbiri yiwemi: kwiba pantchito yayi, kweniso kulimbikira chomene pakagwiriro kantchito. Pala mabwana ghakupenja banthu bantchito, ise tabaku Malawi tikulembeka lubiro kuluskana nabakuno ku South Africa, ba ku Zimbabwe na ku Mozambique. Ndicho chifukwa bakuti tikubapoka ntchito.

(We Malawian migrants are liked by employers in various sectors here in South Africa and this is because of our hard working spirit. Although nowadays jobs are very scarce, we don't struggle a lot in securing jobs and this is also because of a long history and legacy of hard working spirit and trustworthiness that was started by our forefathers. Whenever employers are looking for workers, we, migrants from Malawi, easily get employed as compared to our colleagues from South Africa, Zimbabwe and Mozambique. That is why there are allegations that we snatch their jobs.)

Since the outbreak of xenophobic attacks in 2008 the Malawi government is seen to be reactionary and not proactive in looking after the welfare of its migrant citizens. Instead of being concerned about the plight of Malawian *selufu* migrants since the 1990s, the successive democratic governments are seen to be paying a deaf ear. For instance, following the xenophobic attacks in 2008 and 2015, the Malawi government, after a month or so in each case, was compelled to organize transport to repatriate the affected migrants. However, this came a little late after a number of Malawian migrants had become victims of these attacks: they lost property through looting and even some actually lost their dear lives. After the 2015 attacks the Malawi government made empty promises on the need to establish community skills centres to train Malawians in different fields like tailoring. However, the question here is "why doesn't the Malawi government address the actual cause of labour emigration to South Africa *en masse?*" The main problem is lack of employment and general income-earning opportunities, especially in the countryside. Since the majority of Malawians reside in the countryside, the government is supposed to come up with deliberate initiatives targeting these vulnerable rural dwellers, for instance, building local markets with shops' spaces from where these rural people may operate their grocery shops and other types of businesses.

Each and every year, Malawian migrants based in South Africa end up being abused, attacked and killed by South Africans, but the government does not do anything tangible. However, one would have expected the government to be taking the South African government to task over such developments. Even after being arrested and sent to Lindela Repatriation Centre, the interviewed deported migrants maintain that since the deportation costs are shouldered by the migrants' home governments, other governments are seen to be efficient in ensuring that their migrant citizens do not stay long at Lindela. This is not the case with the Malawi government: the latter is too slow in taking action and, as a result, Malawian migrants spend, say, eight months or even more than a year before transport is arranged by the government to repatriate them to Malawi.

Although labour migrants enter South Africa informally since the early 1990s and also end up working in the informal sector, the government of Malawi is supposed to be concerned with the welfare of its migrant citizens. Despite the fact that during the post-1990 period the Malawi government is not a direct beneficiary of the migrants' working in South Africa, it still remains a beneficiary *de facto*, though indirectly. The proceeds accumulated from their years of working in South Africa are used to develop the migrants' households and societies in Malawi. This leads to the flourishing and growth of rural development centres and trading areas in the labour migrants' source areas. Some of these development initiatives ought to have been masterminded by the government itself in the absence of such initiatives by these migrants. For instance, some of these migrants establish maize mills, groceries, rest houses and other property in their home areas. A good example is the growth of trading centres in areas like Engalaweni, Manyamula, Euthini and Eswazini in Mzimba District and also Chintheche in Nkhata-Bay District.

The other problem that labour migrants are experiencing during their stay in South Africa is lack of work permits. After the expiry of the 30-day visas, they are classified as illegal migrants. This is despite the fact that they enter South Africa as legal migrants with valid passports. This is where the Malawi government is supposed to come to their rescue: negotiating with the South African government for special work permits for all Malawian labour migrants based in South Africa. One of the grounds for such permits would have been the long history of labour migration from Malawi to South Africa. Such initiatives would have borne fruits since there is precedence that such permits were already granted to migrant citizens from other South Africa's neighbouring countries with a similar track record.

In a special meeting with labour officials from Malawi's Consulate Office in South Africa in 2017, the labour officer indicated that Malawi through the Department of Labour was in the process of negotiating with the South African government for the re-opening of *Theba* recruitment operations in Malawi, that is, that Malawian labour migrants be allowed to start going to the South African mines for wage employment. It has to be put on record that since the collapse of *Theba* operations in Malawi in 1988 Malawians, especially former *Wenela* and *Theba* migrants, have been pressurizing the government to negotiate for the resumption of *Theba* recruitment operations. However, the successive governments since 1994 have been paying a deaf year and largely making empty promises to that effect during the general elections every five years.

In 1994 Bakili Muluzi, the first democratically-elected president of Malawi, is on record of having made such promises, arguing "when I become president of Malawi, I will negotiate with South Africa to re-open *Theba*. I don't want you, my people, to be suffering because of lack of employment opportunities". However, after he was duly elected, he vehemently and openly denied having made such promises. Thereafter, most of the print media were awash with this story and one of the newspapers carried a story *"Nkhani yodziwika bwino ya TEBA a Muluzi ayikana"* ("Bakili Mauluzi refutes the well-known TEBA issue"). People were shocked, but like most stories, the issue eventually died down. The issue resurfaced in 1999, and every other five years thereafter, with most political parties taking it up as a campaign matter. Therefore, Malawians are keenly awaiting the outcome of the so-called negotiations on the resumption of the *Theba* issue. However, it is high time the government became serious and stopped politicizing an issue which has a direct bearing on the welfare of a cross-section of households, especially in Malawi's countryside.

As a result of the numerous challenges that Malawian migrants based in South Africa are facing, a group of well-wishing Malawians came together in 2016 and formed, the Malawi Action Group in South Africa (MAGSA), an organization that purports to fight for the improvement in the welfare of fellow Malawians. Its main concern is to lobby with the government of South Africa through Malawi's Consulate Office in Pretoria for the issuance of special work permits to Malawian labour migrants. Once issued, such permits would go a long way in alleviating the plight of Malawian migrants, whose main problem is to secure jobs against a background of expired visas in South Africa.

MAGSA also wishes to conduct civic education among fellow labour migrants in South Africa against the unnecessary harassment by the South African police, immigration officers and Home Affairs officials. MAGSA is against the payment of bribes to such officials. MAGSA is a duly registered body and is recognized by the South African government through the police and Home Affairs Department. It therefore encourages Malawian migrants in South Africa to join its membership and enjoy the privileges of being a MAGSA member: members are given a membership identity card and upon arrest by the police, it is MAGSA which takes over the responsibility of making sure they are freed and this usually happens without payment of the bribes in question. This is a good initiative since most migrants have been suffering in silence and this is largely because of the absence of such legal representation. Since its formation MAGSA membership has been growing rapidly and this proves the fact that Malawian labour migrants across South Africa have seen the significance of being represented in 'an unfair and cruel world'.

Photograph 8: Malawian migrants based in South Africa attending a church session on a Sunday in Berea, Johannesburg. Most Malawian migrants and traders take advantage of such Sunday gatherings to meet their relatives and friends, during which they update each other about developments both in South Africa and at home in Malawi. They usually hold such discussions before and after the church service (photo by author).

Chapter Seven

Conclusion

The book presents some thought-provoking and eye-opening accounts of the experiences of labour migrants and traders of Malawi origin as they make efforts to fulfil their respective migration goals. Chapter one, the first substantive chapter of the book, presents an overview of the history and nature of migration from Malawi to South Africa. It shows that of the two strands, labour migration dates to as far back as the late eighteenth century while commercial migration is a recent phenomenon that can be traced back to the early 1990s. Labour migration, the chapter shows, either took the form of recruited nature or occurred informally. However, both forms existed simultaneously and competed for supremacy. While formal labour migration came to a grinding halt in the 1980s following the HIV wrangle between Malawi and South Africa, informal labour migration or *selufu* continued unabated way into the 1990s and beyond. As for commercial migration, traders started going to South Africa in large numbers after the collapse of the vibrant trade between Malawi and Zimbabwe. This was largely a result of the faltering of the Zimbabwe's once buoyant and vibrant economy. In sharp contrast, the trade between Malawi and Tanzania to the north is both older and still vibrant when compared with trade with Zimbabwe.

In chapter one I also made an attempt to justify the existence of entrenched labour migration from Malawi to South Africa between 1964, the year Malawi attained independence from Britain, to 1994, the year Malawi espoused democratic governance just like South Africa. I argue that one of the reasons for entrenched labour migration to South Africa is the lack of employment opportunities in Malawi as a result of lack of vibrant manufacturing and mining industries. The once strong and reliable manufacturing industries are a thing of the past, courtesy of privatization of government-controlled industries and factories. As a result of this privatization, most of these industries fell into private hands and this had a direct bearing on the quality and amount of goods manufactured. The end result was massive retrenchment of the already poorly-paid workers. The chapter also shows that although the manufacturing industry in Malawi started expanding with the consequent opening of Kayerekera Uranium Mine in Karonga District in northern Malawi, it failed to act as a real catalyst for the creation of the much-needed employment opportunities for a cross-section of Malawians. Hence, contrary to people's expectations, mining in Malawi failed to absorb the repatriated *Wenela* and *Theba* miners. Continued labour emigration is also a direct result of the failure of food and cash crop production to generate financial resources for the majority of Malawians residing in the countryside.

Chapter two presents a detailed account of the challenges that labour migrants and traders of Malawi origin face when traveling between Malawi and South Africa for their respective reasons. While labour migrants goal is to work and accumulate proceeds for use in Malawi, traders' main preoccupation is the making of profit through the buying of *katundu* at wholesale prices in South Africa and later selling them at retail prices in Malawi. Each of these two categories of migrants are interested in fulfilling their set and desired goals. Consequently, labour migrants are ready to overcome problems not only during their stay in South Africa, but also *en route* between Malawi and South Africa. In chapter two I have shown that these labour migrants face challenges of expired visas due to overstaying in South Africa. Although they do overstay in South Africa, these labour migrants face problems in clearing their passports not only within South Africa, but at all the border posts including when going through Zimbabwe and Mozambique. This proves the fact that immigration officials have thrown professionalism to the dogs and their main concern is 'milking' these labour migrants through bribery and corruption.

As for traders, they too face a lot of challenges when traveling between Malawi and South Africa. However, the traders' main problems are not necessarily associated with overstaying in South Africa, rather with high customs duties charged on their already expensive goods. As a result, most traders fail to make the anticipated profits from their otherwise lucrative businesses. The huge custom duty charged on their goods is behind the delays experienced when clearing goods at Malawi's entry posts. This is a result of endless negotiations for either reduced customs duties or informal waivers on selected items. The chapter shows that such delays have a direct bearing on the overall travel period: instead of the normal one and half days, at times the journey from South Africa to Malawi takes two to three days. In short, the chapter shows that while traders are responsible for such delays at Dedza and Mwanza Border Posts, labour migrants are responsible for the delays at Beitbridge either when entering or leaving South Africa.

In chapter three I succinctly argue that the challenges that labour migrants and traders face along the journey to and from South Africa, on the one hand, and the police and immigration officers' willingness to abuse their offices, on the other hand, are fuelling bribery and corruption. The situation is so pathetic that corruption has become institutionalized at almost all borders and road blocks between Malawi and South Africa. On the part of traders, it is this corruption, for instance, when clearing trade goods into Malawi at Mwanza and Dedza border posts, that is behind the untold loss of the much-needed government revenue. Failure to adequately collect this revenue in the long run impedes development activities at societal and national levels within the respective countries. Already with a feeble economy, Malawi, for instance, consequently bears the development pinch. No wonder Malawi has failed to register notable development milestones since the inception of democratic governance in 1994. Similar stories are applicable to corrupt countries like Mozambique and Zimbabwe. As for South Africa, corruption does not have the same impact because it has a strong and vibrant economy in Africa, courtesy of strong mining and manufacturing industries. However, this does not in any way justify corruption tendencies in South Africa.

Chapter three compares the challenges faced by labour migrants and traders *en route* to and from South Africa. It shows that labour migrants face untold problems in trying to enter South Africa mainly at Beitbridge Border Post whereas Malawian male and female traders face more problems not when going to South Africa, but rather when returning to Malawi and, specifically, when trying to clear their trade goods at Mwanza and Dedza Border Posts. Hence their problems are of a different kind. Labour migrants indulge in corrupt practices with immigration and Home Affairs officials while traders enter into shady deals with customs officers. However, the chapter advances the argument that both the sending and receiving countries are affected in various ways by this institutionalized corruption. The labour migrants and traders, themselves, are partly to blame as the institutionalization of this corruption is a direct result of their desperation as they try to enter South Africa and Malawi, respectively.

In chapter four titled "Of Migrants' and Traders' Stay in South Africa" I have examined the various challenges that these labour migrants and traders face during their respective periods of stay in South Africa. Of the two groups, the book shows that it is labour migrants who face greater challenges in view of the fact that they relatively stay longer in South Africa. For instance, their stay usually ranges from a few months to a number of years. Even when the initial plan was to stay briefly in South Africa, most labour migrants end up staying longer on two accounts: first, in trying to maximize the amounts of proceeds since 'the longer the period, the more the accumulated savings' and, second, as a result of the problems in question, for example, as a result of lack of steady and better-paying jobs, labour migrants fail to accumulate enough savings over a short period of time.

In this connection, the chapter has highlighted such challenges as scarcity of jobs which result in other problems like accommodation and food challenges; collapsing of marriages largely because of the unfaithfulness of both husbands and wives during their stay in South Africa; xenophobia; high crime rate; and, last but not least, arrests and deportations as a result of expired visas and lack of working permits. The chapter has shown that scarcity of jobs sweep labour migrants, especially female ones, off their feet so much that they eventually have a problem of survival whilst there in South Africa. In a desperate attempt to 'remain buoyant', they resort to seeking assistance from anything around them that can enable them hang on as they hope to secure jobs. For female labour migrants, this included entering informal love affairs with more established and working fellow Malawian male labour migrants. In most cases, the latter already have wives back in Malawi, but in this case they just look for extra-marital sexual relations. The most interesting part, as highlighted by chapter four, is that each of the two sides has their own obligations and commitments, for instance, dependents like children to support back home. Hence while in such informal marriages, each one of the two partners has their own respective responsibilities to meet. These are, therefore, rightfully termed 'marriages of convenience' and not formal marriages.

In a sad twist, although for many years it was male labour migrants who have been behind the collapsing of marriages, nowadays even wives are associated with dumping husbands once they equally start working in South Africa. For a long time husbands went to South Africa leaving their wives to head households during extended periods of their absence from Malawi. This trend usually resulted in husbands indulging in extra-marital affairs in South Africa and upon their wives discovering this, marriages usually collapsed. This was detrimental to the general welfare and support of their children. This was commonplace during the old labour migration period. Although this practice continued way into the post-1990 period, during this new period a new trend surfaced on the labour migration scene: that of wives accompanying or following their husbands in South Africa. However, after these wives also secure jobs, they become disrespectful to their husbands, with some literally dumping them in favour of other Malawian boyfriends equally working in South Africa. A good number of male labour migrants I interviewed between 2015 And 2017 confessed to me that either their own wives or wives of their close relations were behind the collapse of marriages in question without any befitting reasons.

In chapter five I have examined the fascinating role played by migration in exporting different aspects of Malawian culture abroad. In most cases, scholars highlight the impact of migration on labour migrants in the destination places, showing how these migrants end up adopting foreign cultures. These aspects of foreign cultures end up in Malawi when migrants are returning home. This chapter has, however, argued that these Malawian migrants, though in minority, impact on the lives of the local people in the destination areas. They spread aspects of their own culture, for instance, language, dressing and traditional dances. The chapter has advanced this argument by citing examples of this kind of impact in South Africa. Other scholars have also highlighted such an impact in other areas, for instance, in Zimbabwe.

Chapter six has highlighted the contrasting roles played by the government during the old and new migration periods. During the old period, the chapter has shown, the government was actively intervening for the improved working conditions of Malawian labour migrants, especially those who were working in the South African mines. This was largely because the government saw itself as a direct beneficiary of the labour migration process. However, with the collapse of the formal and recruited migration in the 1980s and the consequent escalation of *selufu* from the early 1990s onwards, the government has been rather passive in its involvement. Government's involvement, however, comes to the surface following waves of xenophobic attacks in South Africa. This was clearly seen in 2008 and 2015. However, the government is largely seen to be reactive: coming in to assist rather late when Malawian migrants have already suffered a great deal and when others have lost their precious lives. As a way forward, in this chapter I argue in favour of active government involvement since even during the new period the government stands to benefit from the labour migrants' proceeds from the informal wage employment in South Africa.

Photograph 9: A number of foreign workers including Malawian migrants cannot afford decent housing in South Africa because of expensive accommodation against a background of low wages. Consequently, they are forced to "squat" in high density residential areas where they rent *mikhukhu* ("shacks") as can be seen from this photograph (photo by author).

Photograph 10: *Malipenga* dance in action. *Malipenga* is a popular cultural dance of the Tonga from Nkhata-Bay District in northern Malawi (see map of Malawi below). However, the dance is also performed in other lakeshore districts like Rumphi and Karonga in northern Malawi. The dancers traditionally put on white attire: white shirts, shorts and shoes. During *malipenga* dance, the women's role is to sing and 'offer morale' while men are dancing (source: https://www.tiunike.com/photo-gallery).

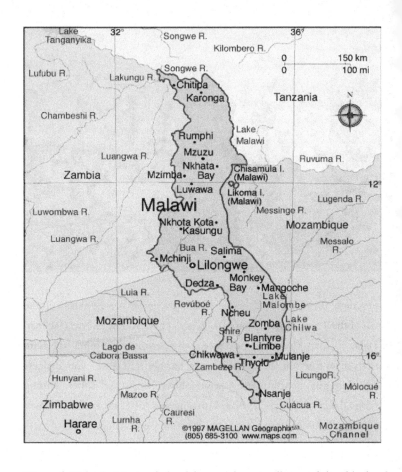

Map of Malawi: Most of the labour migrants discussed in this book originate from the northern region districts of Mzimba and Nkhata-Bay, the two districts historically associated with formal and informal migration history to South Africa in northern Malawi. These migrants mainly depart for South Africa from Mzuzu City. Although traders also come from these two districts, other traders originate from Lilongwe, the Capital City. Buses and lorries from Mzuzu and Lilongwe exit at Dedza Border Post while those from Blantyre exit at Mwanza Border Post. Mwanza District is next to Chikwawa in southern Malawi (source: google maps).

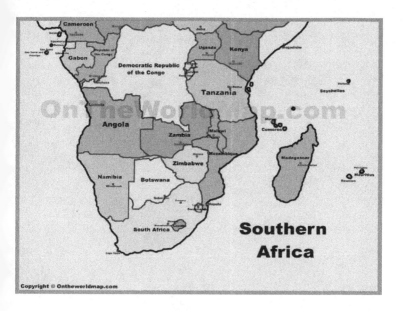

Map of Southern Africa: Labour migrants and traders start off from Mzuzu (northern Malawi), Lilongwe (Capital City, central Malawi) or Blantyre (southern Malawi) either by lorries operated by local transporters or by coaches like Intercape, Munorurama and Chipozani. From there they go through Mozambique and Zimbabwe before entering South Africa mainly through Beitbridge Border Post. In total, they cross six border posts. This journey usually takes around thirty six hours, that is, one and half days (source: Google maps).

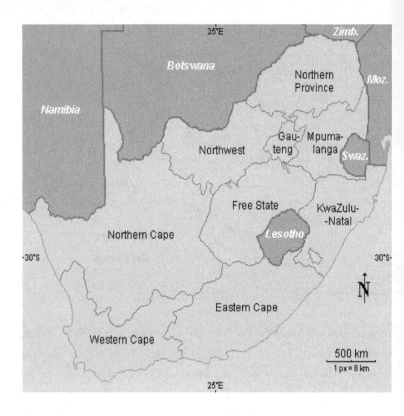

Map of South Africa showing provinces: The ultimate destination for the majority of labour migrants discussed in this book is Johannesburg in Gauteng Province. This is mainly because of the convenience in transport when traveling to and from South Africa: Park Station, the major transport hub and the source and destination of almost all buses is in Johannesburg. However, because of the scarcity of jobs in Gauteng, since the 2000s some labour migrants seek jobs in outlying provinces. Almost all traders also end up in Johannesburg, the commercial hub of South Africa (source: Google maps).

Printed in the United States
By Bookmasters